The Kaleidoscope

KALEIDOSCOPE

God's Patterns in the
Bits and Pieces of Our Lives

CLAIRE CLONINGER

WORD BOOKS
PUBLISHER
WACO, TEXAS

A DIVISION OF

Unless otherwise indicated, Scripture quotations in this book are from *The New American Standard Bible,* © The Lockman Foundation 1960, 1962, 1963, 1968, 1971, 1972, 1973, 1975, 1977. Quotations marked PHILLIPS are from the 1958 edition of *The New Testament in Modern English* by J. B. Phillips, published by the Macmillan Company, © 1958, 1960, 1972 by J. B. Phillips. Quotations marked LB are from *The Living Bible,* copyright 1971 by Tyndale House Publishers, Wheaton, IL, used by permission. Quotations marked NKJV are from the New King James Version, copyright © 1979, 1980, 1982, Thomas Nelson, Inc., Publisher. Quotations marked KJV are from the King James Version of the Bible.

Library of Congress Cataloging-in-Publication Data:

Cloninger, Claire.
    The Kaleidoscope: God's patterns in the bits and pieces of our lives.

    1. Christian life—1960–   . 2. Women—Religious
life.   3. Cloninger, Claire.   I. Title.
BV4501.2.C588   1988   248.4   88-10672
ISBN 0-8499-0625-3

Printed in the United States of America

8 9 8 0 1 2 3 9 RRD 9 8 7 6 5 4 3 2 1

To Jenny, Katie, and Radcliff
You are not forgotten.

Contents ✸

Acknowledgments ✤

OCCASIONALLY IN MY songwriting career, I have had a song that just seemed to "happen." It seemed to drop down out of the sky and into my typewriter.

Books don't just happen. No way. I owe special thanks to a dear group of folks who labored with me to get this manuscript into its final form. To my editor at Word, Anne Buchanan, for her hard work and encouragement. To Mama, John, Laura, Marshall, and Mary Lou for reading, research, and reassurance. To Debbie, Val, and Don at Word for giving me time off from songwriting.

To my Christ Church "family" and my Bible study group for your prayers. To my husband, Spike; my children, Curt and Andy; and my parents, Charlie and Virginia, for your love and support.

And especially to Jesus for the light!

The Kaleidoscope ✺

Have you ever thought of life as a kaleidoscope?

Revelation in a Pigpen 1
Discovering the Kaleidoscope Principle

"I FELL INTO BED last night so exhausted I could hardly breathe!" The exasperated voice on the phone was that of my friend Mallie, mother of four. "I'll bet I had put three hundred miles on my van by the time the sun went down yesterday—and I never even went out of Spring Hill."

Wearily she recounted the litany of her daily rounds: "Two carpools, grocery store, ballet lessons, boy scouts, dentist appointment, and a birthday party. You know, I'm beginning to feel that my van and I have a lot in common. We're both jerked in this direction, then that direction, then back again, and neither one of us seems to be getting anywhere."

My usually optimistic friend was dealing with what I consider one of the major down sides of twentieth-century living—that helpless feeling of fragmentation.

Anne Morrow Lindbergh observed somewhere in her timeless little book, *Gift from the Sea*, that women don't really mind pouring their lives out for a reason. What they do resent is the feeling that it is being dribbled away in small, meaningless drops to no avail. For me, probably the greatest frustration of walking through the "dailiness" of life as a Christian wife and mother is that I hardly ever get to see how the bits and pieces of my efforts fit together into the big picture of God's plan. It's tempting at times to see my life as a meal here, a meeting there, a carpool, a phone call, a sack of groceries—all disjointed fragments of nothing in particular.

And yet I know I am called, as God's child, to believe by faith that they do add up. That in some way every single scrap of my life, every step and every struggle, is in the process of being

15

fitted together into God's huge and perfect pattern for good (Rom. 8:28). As difficult as that is to "live into" on a daily basis, it is becoming for me a transforming truth, adding meaning to the mundane and purpose to the plodding!

There was a particular morning one October when a window in my spirit was thrown open to this idea. That morning, I was doing a rare thing—I was "tidying up" in Andy's room.

Does every family have an Andy? He is our bright-eyed, easy-going free spirit who has never quite made the connection between toy and toy box, book and bookshelf, T-shirt and drawer. Consequently, most of the time his room looks like it would qualify for federal aid to disaster areas. (I remember once we were trying to decide where to house a lovely old English missionary gentleman who was coming to visit. My husband, Spike, thought for a while and decided, "If he liked Africa, he'll love Andy's room. He could get lost in there for days!")

So on this particular October morning, having entered the wilds of Andy's domain with courage and resolve, I had begun my semiannual shoveling out. I had not been at it long when I happened upon one of those enchanting little cardboard kaleidoscopes of the dime-store variety. All progress ceased as I stood for who-knows-how-long at the open window, totally preoccupied with the intricate, jewel-like patterns that shifted and changed as I turned the cardboard cylinder.

I remember I was thinking, *How beautiful* . . . , when it suddenly hit me. What I was looking at through that tiny peephole was really nothing more than broken glass. Yet when the morning light came through at a certain angle, my eyes could see . . . diamonds!

I knew then with utter clarity that I was holding in my hand a metaphor for my own life in Christ. For when the light of His life shines through the brokenness of my own, He can transform all the scattered, disjointed pieces into something very beautiful.

Since that day, I have been helped more times than I can count by remembering that I serve a God who is in the business of shining through the seemingly insignificant pieces of my life and using them to form patterns that are pleasing to Him. Looking at life through the colorful perspective of this simple little metaphor is helping me daily to discover countless new and exciting ways to accept and even embrace the fragmented quality of my life.

When I view the work and worry, the routines and relationships of my days as the glass (small, broken, disjointed pieces, brightly colored and transparent), I learn helpful truths about what my life can be in Christ.

When I view Christ as the light, as Scripture certainly does (John 1:4–5), light that brings warmth and healing, light that illumines truth and offers guidance, I understand what power He is able and willing to bring into the confusion of each small moment.

And when I view my daily circumstances as the cylinder of the kaleidoscope, the container which holds the bright fragments of my life, I thrill again and again to see the way His light shines into those circumstances, decorating my days with the beautiful, redemptive patterns of His love.

Kaleidoscope

I found a child's kaleidoscope
And held it to the light,
I watched the patterns come and go
Like diamonds in the night,
And, Jesus, then it dawned on me
Exactly what your love can be.

(Chorus)
You shine your life through mine,
Making beautiful designs
Out of all the broken pieces that you find.
And Lord, when you shine through,
Just look what love can do —
You make diamonds out of bits of broken glass,
Out of all the broken pieces of my past!

I know that, Jesus, you're the light,
And I'm the broken glass,
My life is the kaleidoscope
Through which the light must pass,
Now suddenly my eyes can see
The patterns of your love for me.

(Repeat Chorus)

(Bridge)
Turning and changing in color and line,
Images sparkle in shifting design
Like rainbows unfolding each new day I see
The colors of your life come shining through me.

(Repeat Chorus)

Like the bits of glass in the kaleidoscope,
our lives are <u>*small.*</u>

Sister to a Mustard Seed 2
Sizing Up Our Lives

ACTOR KIRK DOUGLAS told in a recent interview about picking up a sailor who was hitchhiking outside Palm Springs. The sailor got in the car, took one look at Douglas, and blurted out, "Hey! Do you know who you are?"[1]

Funny story—but at times that question can be a really hard one for me. I tend to forget who I am, especially who I am in relation to God. I get out of touch with my size and importance in relation to His. I get so involved in the particulars of my own small world that I unconsciously begin to view myself as the leading character in my own little soap opera, rather than as a supporting character in God's great drama of life. I find myself living as though I were a totally autonomous being in control of my own destiny, rather than the child of a loving God living by His grace.

It is very humbling to have to acknowledge my real size in the great scheme of things, to admit that, like those bits of broken glass in the kaleidoscope, my life is really quite small. In my prayer times, I have sometimes been guilty of de-emphasizing the awesome majesty of God and concentrating instead on how lovingly accessible He is to me—a much more comfortable perspective. Viewing Him as my own personal "prayer partner" rather than the high and mighty Ruler of the universe has allowed me during those times to operate as though I were in control of Him rather than the other way around.

I love the poem by Yorifumi Yaguchi which so eloquently indicts all of us who have been guilty of this offense:

We trap God
hang Him
In stained glass
entrance Him
by organ music
and chorus

We bind Him
by ritual
tickle Him
by prayers
and train Him
to become our pet.

. . .

Once the desert God
jealous
and wild
now an amulet
on a charm
bracelet[2]

SMALL BUT VALUABLE

We never really know who we are until we see our size and importance in relation to His. David got a glimpse of this in Psalm 8, and it "blew him away":

> When I consider Thy heavens, the work of Thy fingers,
> The moon and the stars, which Thou hast ordained;
> What is man, that Thou dost take thought of him?
> And the son of man, that Thou dost care for him?
>
> (vv. 3–4).

I remember years ago taking our two young sons to a concert of the music group, "Kansas." That group's big hit at the time was a beautiful, haunting ballad by Kerry Livgren called "Dust in the Wind," which repeated over and over the mournful line, "All we are is dust in the wind." It is a chilling thought to view one's life as a mere speck of dust being swirled without meaning through time and space. The lyric puts me in mind of the writer of Ecclesiastes, who sees his smallness in the scheme of things and concludes that his quest for meaning has amounted to nothing more than "striving after wind" (Eccles. 1:17).

Coming to grips with the fact of my smallness in relation to God's enormity is destined to be depressing unless I also grasp, as David did, that God does care for me—very much. I am small, yes. But I am assured all through Scripture that small things matter tremendously to God.

Even the most minute details of my life are of enormous importance to Him. He carefully chose and assembled every part of my being in my mother's womb (Ps. 139:13), and He even knows the number of hairs on my head (Matt. 10:30). He calls me to come to Him *as a little child*, cautioning that any other spiritual condition will result in my failure to gain the kingdom (Matt. 18:3). He invites me to cast every single concern of my heart (even the small ones) upon Him, because He cares for me so intimately (1 Peter 5:7). He is a God who grieves over every falling sparrow (Matt. 10:29) and who sees the essence of the kingdom in a tiny mustard seed (Matt. 13:31). Understanding these things about God helps me to realize that smallness cannot be equated with unimportance in His sight, for small things matter greatly to Him.

Some years ago, I was asked by my friend Martha to pinch-hit as teacher of a neighborhood Bible study she was holding for high-school girls. I was unable to plan my lesson until the afternoon of the night I was to teach. Feeling a little desperate, I asked the Lord to show me a topic that would matter to those girls. Just as I finished praying, my eye was caught by a *Life* magazine on the coffee table lying open to a picture of the current teen "heart-throb," John Travolta. I read with interest the story of Travolta's rise to stardom, as well as his confession that fame had brought with it new tensions and a tendency to stay isolated from others. He was pictured with his expensive automobiles and other luxurious possessions against the backdrop of his spacious California ranch. And it seemed to me that behind the handsome features of this famous face, there was a real loneliness.

I flipped through the magazine and, just a few pages away, found a second article of interest. It was a story and picture layout of Mother Teresa and her ministry to the "poorest of the poor" in India. Here was the tale of a young girl who left her native Albania, drawn by a calling to serve God in India. After becoming a nun and teaching for several years in India, her heart was drawn to help the poor, the homeless, and the dying that she saw all around her. She had no master plan and certainly no desire for fame. She merely began to meet the need closest at hand, caring for one destitute or dying person at a time, until within a matter of years a great international ministry had grown up around her. When the Nobel Committee selected this petite nun to receive its coveted award, no one could have been more surprised than the recipient herself. She had never sought nor anticipated the international acclaim that came to her.

I remember especially one photograph in the article, a close-up of Mother Teresa's weathered face. In it she was totally surrendered to the laughter of an unguarded moment. The expression of joy captured on film was so contagious that it was almost impossible for me to look at the picture without chuckling a little myself.

Here were two stories about two famous people whose lives had affected and influenced their world. What was the difference? I closed the magazine satisfied that I had all I needed to involve the girls in a wonderful discussion on values, commitment, and lifestyle.

Most of us probably will never be written up in *Life* magazine. Yet each of us, like these two celebrities, is given only one small life. We can choose to deny our human frailty and try to forge our own path through its pain and difficulties, singing with Frank Sinatra as we go, "I did it my way." Or we can see and agree with our own smallness and choose the Lord's way, allowing Him to "go ahead of us" to clear the path (Deut. 31:8).

EMBRACING OUR CREATURELINESS

Susan Annette Muto, in her challenging book on the Beatitudes, suggests that real freedom lies in our ability to agree with our own smallness, accepting the "reality of who we are as limited creatures." "False freedom," on the other hand, "tries to deny this sense of creatureliness." She suggests that when we are in agreement with and compassionate toward our own limitations and vulnerability, we are most likely to begin to transcend them.[3]

When I think of learning to accept our "creatureliness," I am reminded of something that happened one sweltering August in Mobile when our then-eleven-year-old son Curt was suffering through daily football practices in one hundred-plus degree weather. One early evening after practice he appeared in my room—filthy, sweaty, and smelling as only an eleven-year-old boy can smell, but wearing an enormous smile.

"I just figured something out," he said, plopping his grubby little body down on my bedspread. (We learned early with this introspective child that when he figures something out, we'd best listen, 'cause it's gonna be good!)

"I was walking up to practice, and it was so hot," he began. "I just kept wondering to myself why do I do it. I mean, I know that I'm going to get knocked down, and get hot and tired and beat up, but I still keep on going to practice. Why?"

"I don't know," I answered. "Why?"

"Well that part was easy. I play football so I can prove I'm good, just like I study so I can make good grades and prove I'm good. You know?"

I nodded. "I know." (Boy did I!)

"But here's the other part. After practice I was walking home through the park. The sky was turning red behind the pine trees, and all the bugs were making noise, and I heard this little katydid clacking his wings somewhere down by my feet. I looked, and there he was flipped over on his back, trying to turn himself over, making a big fuss. So I got this stick and I just sort of gave him a little flip. He was so glad. He clacked his wings harder than ever like he was trying to thank me. And it was weird, Mom."

"What was weird?"

"Well, it was like I knew something I never knew before. I knew that I was just like that katydid. I didn't have to play football or make *A*s or prove anything to anybody. I'm supposed to be here just like the katydid. I belong here, 'cause God made me.'

I had to gulp back my tears. What an experience of grace! Becoming aware of his own "creatureliness" gave Curt a wonderful sense of belonging in the world, as well as the freedom to be his real self without having to prove anything.

Embracing our "creatureliness" is one way to show God that we value the "small life" He has given us—with its limitations and its potential. The extent to which God Himself values a human life is seen most clearly when we look at the Incarnation. It is fascinating to consider the fact that two thousand years ago God Himself chose to live out one of these "small lifetimes" alongside us. He purposely went outside of His own enormity and entered into our smallness. He chose to take on every human limitation of our flesh:

> Although He existed in the form of God, [Jesus] did not regard equality with God a thing to be grasped, but emptied Himself, taking the form of a bond-servant, and being made in the likeness of men (Phil. 2:6–7).

Jesus certainly could have opted for the spiritual power play, arriving on lightening bolts and zapping whole cities with a single word. Instead, he arrived in one of the most fragile and vulnerable packages in the world, the body of a newborn baby. He grew up in a family, learned a trade, went to temple like other Jewish boys, and didn't even "get down to business" until he was thirty years old. Then he traveled by foot, spoke to a few thousand people (often one at a time), discipled a handful of followers, and died an inglorious death. He was pleased enough, however, with the results of His small-scope ministry to say from the cross, "It is finished."

A HUMBLE HEART

When we examine the life and teachings of Jesus, it is interesting to note how frequently He encourages us to adopt the heart position of the small and humble. We are told that the least person shall be the greatest (Luke 9:48), that to be faithful with a small number of things will result in our being put in charge of a large number of things (Matt. 25:21), and even that to minister to the "least of men" constitutes ministry to the Lord Himself (Matt. 25:40). Indeed, the hallmark of the Lord's very life was His desire to identify with the humble, the needy, the destitute. And the heart of His message to us who would follow after Him is that we must be willing to do the same.

So often we rush out in our fervent desire to do "great things" for the kingdom, forgetting the necessary first step of ministry —which is a humble heart-attitude before the Lord. I believe that many well-intended plans have gone awry in the church today because of our misplaced emphasis on the size and greatness of our endeavors. We become carried away with the number of converts filling the pews and the amounts listed on pledge cards, forgetting that the first focus of our Lord is not upon the grand scale of our efforts, but upon the humbleness and obedience of every heart that comes to Him.

Numbers did not concern our Lord when He was on earth. He left us the example of a life which touched and responded to others person-to-person.

(This is certainly not to suggest that the Lord is opposed to large numbers of converts. It is, however, to suggest that He is concerned first and foremost with the heart attitude which motivates the ministry and with the love we bring to the lost, whatever their number. As our pastor, John Barr, says frequently, "The Lord said, 'feed My sheep,' not 'count My sheep'!")

Once our hearts and wills have been surrendered to and lined up with His, great numbers and impressive results *may* follow—or they may not. Either way, we can be certain that, if our heart attitude is right, the outcome will be pleasing to Him. "God sees not as man sees, for man looks at the outward appearance, but the Lord looks at the heart" (1 Sam. 16:7).

THE PULL OF THE POWERFUL

But it's not easy to keep our hearts focused on the small, inglorious tasks that the Lord has for us all. We tend to want to do "important" jobs and let someone else worry about the small stuff. As Sue Garmon puts it,

> Lord, I want so much to do
> BIG things for you.
> I'd like so much
> to make a grand gesture,
> to do something
> really spectacular.
> Something BIG.
>
> But you don't ask me
> to do things like that.
> You ask me to do
> the little piddling things
> that make up my everyday life.
> You don't ask me to do something
> grand and glorious;

just to do my job.
You don't ask me
to do something really spectacular;
just to love my neighbor.
You don't ask me
to do something
absolutely stupendous;
just the routine,
day-in, day-out duties
of a working woman.

Lord, when I feel
that what I'm doing
is insignificant
and unimportant,
help me to remember
that everything I do
is significant
and important
in your eyes,
because you love me
and you put me here,
and no one else
can do what I am doing
in exactly the way
I do it. . . . [4]

One of Satan's oldest and most attractive temptations is to lure us out of the realm of the small and obedient walk with a promise of greatness and power. In the wilderness, Satan tried three ways to pull Jesus away from His commitment to operate within human limitations. He knew very well who Jesus was—and that He was infinitely capable of making bread from stone, of jumping off cliffs without a scratch, of commanding the worship of nations with the bat of an eyelash.

But Jesus had come to live as a Son, to do only what He heard His Father saying to Him (John 5:19–20, 30). He had come to demonstrate the love and power of a limitless God operating within a limited human vessel. And it was precisely this plan that Satan sought to destroy. If he could persuade Jesus to operate as an independent agent, God's blueprint for salvation would be shredded.

"Why should you have to be bogged down in the small details of life?" he whispered to Jesus. "Why should you have to concern yourself with things like hunger or gravity or loneliness? Take action on your own, and you'll be fed, you'll be invincible, you'll be worshiped."

It was the same voice that had whispered to Eve, "Why should you be content within the limits of the garden, within the limits of your own knowledge? Eat this, and you'll be like God."

And it is the same voice that whispers to us today, "Why should you have to sweat the small stuff? Why should you get bogged down in somebody else's antiquated notions of morality? Times have changed. You've come a long way, baby. You've got to get out there and forge your own destiny. Make it happen! Fulfill yourself! Pull your own strings! Do it your way!"

CAUGHT IN THE "ME TRAP"

There was a time when I listened to that voice and nearly lost myself. I recognize it now as the voice of spiritual rebellion, whose purpose is to drown out God's quiet call to righteousness.

Righteousness is sometimes defined as being in right relation to God. And what exactly is right relation? Quite simply, it is acknowledging my utter dependence on Him—that I am powerless, whereas He is all-powerful; that I am needy, whereas He is all-sufficient; or, in the words of the old Sunday school classic, that "I am weak but He is strong." Until I came to this exact point of surrender in my Christianity, God was thwarted in His ability to operate fully in my life.

I remember clearly the night that I was finally able to accept these realities with abandon. Somebody once said that you come to the foot of the cross at the end of your rope. I know that on that freezing January night in 1977, I was in both places at once. I came to this spiritual juncture on the carpeted hallway floor of our Mobile, Alabama, home. The rest of my family was sound asleep, and I was sitting there going through what is sometimes referred to as a "dark night of the soul." I know now that I was wrestling with the Lord that night as surely as Jacob once did (Gen. 32:24–30). And the bone of contention was this: Who is in charge here?

I had been hearing a rumor for a number of years—that Jesus Christ was interested in being my Savior *and* my Lord. I had already come, thanks to His grace, into the "Savior" part of the transaction; I knew that I needed one of those.

But "Lord"! I understood the implications of the word *Lord,* and I wanted no part of it. It meant that Somebody Else would be in control, and I had always insisted on being in control myself. Only it seemed that, especially lately, things were not working out very well with me in control.

I had fallen into the "ME Trap" set by the world. I had totally bought into its propaganda that says a woman must seek and find "fulfillment" at all costs.

Now, please understand, I'm still a big believer in fulfillment. I believe we each have a responsibility to fulfill our unique potential as God's children—to discover and develop our God-given gifts. But the message I was getting from the world was quite different from that. The essence of this message (at least my thoroughly selfish interpretation of it) was that I should roll over whatever got in *my* way to get what was *my* birthright as a human being—"fulfillment." Life owed it to *me,* and I was going after it. I had become a "gusto grabber." Everything was expendable—husband, children, home. Nothing was to keep *me* from what I deserved. I spent the better part of five years doing this insane do-si-do with my ego, going back and forth, trying this, that, and everything to fill up the vacuum inside.

Like a top gone wild, I went spinning off in all directions on my quest. But though some things worked for a while, nothing seemed able to satisfy for very long this crazy restlessness in me. I tried community service in a big way, joining every organization and serving on every board that came to my attention. (Saying no was impossible for me in those days.) I also took voice lessons and dance class and worked part-time performing with a professional acting troupe that took children's theater productions into local schools. I even considered going back to school to work on another degree. (I already had a master's and twelve hours' work toward my Ph.D. that I wasn't using for anything in particular.)

I remember one day when I was leaving my house with a load of scripts in one arm and a dance bag over the other, our little Andy looked up into my face with his perfectly clear blue eyes and asked so sincerely, "Mommy, what are you going to be when you grow up?" Now that was a great question for me. The kid was really on to something, because I was light years from any kind of emotional or spiritual maturity.

I now know that on that cold January night I was coming to the end of my frantic season of "questing" after fulfillment and taking perhaps my first halting step toward "growing up." That night I began coming to terms with the sad realization that during my "quest" I had managed to hurt or damage or neglect almost everybody I really cared about. The truth was painful but evident. When you spend twenty-four hours of every day seeking to fulfill yourself, you end up pretty full of yourself!

Now it seemed as though everything solid in my life, everything I had taken for granted, was falling apart in my hands. I did not have a healthy relationship to my name, including my marriage. I had nothing to show for all this restless thrashing about but an enormous well of loneliness inside. It's hard to describe all that I was feeling that night. I was scared to death, for one thing, because I knew that everything wrong in my life was my fault, and I couldn't fix it. I hurt. That was the main feeling—tremendous emotional pain.

So there I sat on the floor alone, at the end of my rope and at the foot of the cross, in need of a Savior again. But this time it was different. This time I knew instinctively that I couldn't fool around anymore. I knew that I had better be ready either to talk commitment with the Lord or to quit. And if I quit, there was no other place to go.

MY HEART'S DESIRE

I had my Bible with me that night, which was pretty unusual. The Bible was one thing I had definitely given up during my "quest." But in my desperation that night, I had decided to blow the dust off of the old Book and try it again. Playing "Scripture roulette," I flipped from place to place, not finding anything very helpful at first. That was when one little verse caught my eye.

(You know how it is when the Lord is speaking to you— suddenly there are flashing neon lights around something. Usually it's something that's been there all along, only now you see it as you've never seen it before.)

The verse said, "Delight yourself in the Lord; and He will give you the desires of your heart" (Ps. 37:4). The desires of my heart? I read it over again, and it was the funniest thing. That was the first time I think I ever realized that I had not the vaguest notion of what "the desires of my heart" might be.

"Delight yourself in the Lord, and He will give you the desires of your heart."

Too easy, I thought. *There's got to be a catch. . . . Oh, yeah. I get it. I delight in You. Then You* become *the desires of my heart. Then You give me You, and we all live boringly ever after. No. Uh-uh. Not me.*

And yet I couldn't turn the page. Somehow I knew that in that verse there was a key to my restless longing. That was when it came to me. God must know something about *me* that *I* didn't know!

All of a sudden, I was so in touch with my smallness and His greatness. My unworthiness and His worthiness. My neediness and His sufficiency to meet that need. This is what came to me that night and washed over me like a great wave:

If the Lord is the One who made this heart of mine, maybe He is the only One who understands my real desires. Maybe He even programed them into me, knowing that they would finally drive me to my knees in search of Him. And maybe He is the only One who can fulfill them!

A RUSTY PRAYER—A NEW BEGINNING

I prayed a simple prayer that night, the rusty kind of prayer that comes from a heart that's "been away" for a while. I think I said something like this:

Lord, I'm not sure why You want me. But I believe You do want me. I don't know what You're going to do with me when You get me. But You've got me. 'Cause Lord, *I've tried every other thing I could think of,* and nothing worked. So now I'm ready to try You.

Did it ever occur to you what a really great sport the Lord is? I mean, what if I were a high-school girl who got a call one night from a guy in my class, and this guy had the audacity to say to me, "Hello, Claire. I've just tried every other girl I could think of, and no one else can go. So how 'bout you?" Boy! I'd hang up so fast it would make your head swim!

But praise God! The Lord isn't like that. He finds us where we're hurting, and He takes us where He finds us—no questions asked. Once we're ready to confess our sins and His Lordship,

He's ready to "gather up the pieces" of our lives. Just as He did with the loaves and the fish, He can make our bits and pieces into "infinitely more than we ever dare to ask or imagine" (Eph. 3:20, PHILLIPS).

That night was, for me, the beginning of a beautiful new life in Christ. It has not always been characterized by easy answers or smooth sailing. But it has certainly been a life rich with meaning, vibrant with power, and saturated with His grace. In Him, I am growing in my ability to deal with the unpredictable and fragmented qualities of my daily circumstances. I am learning to delight in my smallness and His greatness, for this is the key to a righteous (right) relationship with Him. And the more I delight in the Lord, the more He gives to me the desires of my heart. The *real* desires. The ones which fulfill this heart which He created for Himself.

LORD JESUS, thank You that You came to be Savior and Lord. Thank you that real freedom comes from surrendering to Your love, and real fulfillment comes from being filled full of You. Open our hearts to the reality that though our lives are small, there are no limits to what You can accomplish in us. Fill our hearts with the celebration of Your new and unending life. We worship and praise You, and we pray in Your precious name. AMEN.

Simple Song for a Mighty God

He spread the stars across the night
And built His palace in the heavens.
On a chariot of clouds He rode the wind.
He set the earth on its foundations,
Turning slowly through forever—
Do I dare to praise a God as great as Him?

(Chorus)
If a simple song can please a mighty God,
Then I will sing my song to Him.
If a simple song can please a mighty God,
Then I must simply praise Him!

Wrapped in robes of light,
He brought creation into being—
All the birds of song and fishes of the sea.
He made every living thing
That walks the fields and roams the forests;
Still He bends His ear to hear a song from me!

(Repeat Chorus)

(Bridge)
And if my song is pleasing, I will sing
Of all the suns and moons and seasons
That His breath of life can bring.

(Repeat Chorus)

Like the bits of glass in the kaleidoscope,
our lives are <u>disjointed</u>.

My Favorite Christine 3
When Things Won't Hold Together

WHEN I WAS LITTLE, all of my dolls were named either Sally or Christine—don't ask me why. All the cute ones—the rag dolls and baby dolls and pudgy toddler walking dolls—were Sally. But the glamorous dolls, the ones in evening gowns with little fur jackets carefully stitched by my talented grandmother, Mimi, or the bride dolls who arrived with Mimi-made trousseaus in tiny trunks—those were the Christines.

My favorite Christine was a flaxen-haired Toni doll that I loved literally to pieces. When I finally retired her to a cardboard carton of cherished playthings in my mother's attic, the rubber band that once held her shapely limbs to her shapely torso had totally relaxed, leaving a sad stack of disjointed pieces not unlike Ezekiel's dry bones.

But about six years ago, my mom did for Christine what all the king's horses and all the king's men could not do for Humpty Dumpty. She gathered up those pieces of my favorite Christine and took them in a box to her neighbor, Miss Lucy Meaux, a woman we always referred to as "the doll lady" because of her in-house doll museum and "hospital." Imagine my grown-up joy on Christmas morning at finding Christine restrung, rewigged, and glamorously refrocked in dotted Swiss and lace under the Christmas tree!

I wonder if you've ever felt a little bit like my favorite Christine (before her trip to Miss Lucy's, that is). I feel that way so many times. By nightfall some days I feel like a stack of disjointed pieces with no hope of ever being restrung. I've gone from person to problem to thing all day long with no sense of

41

continuity and very little feeling of accomplishment. All of the concerns of my day seem to lie unsorted at my feet like those disordered and disconnected bits of glass in the kaleidoscope. And if I let myself, I could fling myself down among them in an incoherent heap!

Take yesterday, for instance. It went something like this:

(1)   Made breakfast and sack lunch for Andy. Cleaned up.

(2)   Tried to have quiet time (multiple interruptions).

(3)   Ran half a mile of a two-mile course. Pulled something in my hip and hobbled home.

(4)   Kept appointment with school principal to discuss Andy's grades and ways to help.

(5)   Had van washed and waxed just in time to get caught in a rainstorm.

(6)   Had prescription filled at drugstore.

(7)   Went to downtown bank to acquire copies of deposit slips for IRS audit (oh, joy!).

(8)   Celebrated birthday lunch with Fran (her fiftieth!).

(9)   Shopped for certain kind of shorts requested by Curt for his college cross-country team (no luck finding them).

(10)   Picked up baptism Bibles for the Kelly children at bookstore.

(11)   Answered calls on phone machine (Nancy, Gerrit, Morris, Sewanee Parent Committee).

(12)   Cooked two kinds of dinner (Andy is trying to "body build" for football; Spike is on a diet.) Ate with Spike and Andy—some from each menu!

(13)   Cleaned kitchen. Again.

(14)   Folded clothes while taking several calls (Laura, Kitty, Lynn K. from Word).

(15)   Escaped to office to work for thirty minutes on new lyric, "Midnight Sun."

(16)   Fell asleep watching the end of a movie with Spike (I'm not even positive what it was called, though ironically enough I think it was titled, *That's Life!*)

I sincerely hope you didn't stop reading this book just because I bored you to death telling you about my day! It was not a spectacular day—I know that. It was lovely in spots (my lunch with Fran). It was irritating in spots (the rain on the freshly washed van). But mostly it was just "daily." So daily.

DEALING WITH THE DAILY

Sometimes in the middle of a "daily" sort of a day like yesterday, something in me rises up and can't help thinking, *There is so much I want to be doing! There are so many things I want to say in my songs. And I'm yearning to finish writing this book that I've only just started. But instead, the real bulk of my time seems to be spent dealing with the interruptions—coping, managing, getting through, putting out little, daily "brush fires" that spring up all around me, instead of really making a difference.*

I feel some days like I'm drowning in the meaningless minutia of daily living instead of swimming in the brisk, exhilarating current of that "abundant life" Jesus has promised (John 10:10).

On a "daily" sort of day like yesterday, it is very difficult for me to discern any sort of order or power or meaning operating in this hodgepodge of activity. If there's a purpose in any of these things I'm doing, I have a hard time seeing it.

And yet I know (by faith) that there is a purpose! I know that just a prayer away from my spiritual thirst is a great reservoir of living water available for me to tap into. Just beyond the frustrations of my "dailiness" there is enough grace and power to transform a handful of glass into a diamond tiara!

What is the mystery that I speak of, the miracle that I have uncovered, the extraordinary answer capable of lifting the ordinary life out of its humdrum reality? I'm sorry (and thrilled) to inform you that I have no new answers—only an old, infinitely meaningful one. For every answer I know to every question I ask begins with letting the Lord be in control—putting the reins of my life into His strong hands and leaving them there. There is a real bottom line to the Christian journey—and this is it. We human beings are destined to be trapped in the transient trivia of this world until we are willing to step over into the eternal perspective of His indwelling life.

Scripture tells us that only in Christ Jesus was everything designed to hold together (Col. 1:15–17). All "pieces," all fragments, all frustrations, all loose ends of a life that frequently feels "frayed"—only in Him do they fit and knit together and fall into place. He is the glue of the human heart. And just as our beings have sprung from His being, our

meaning and purpose must spring from His, if we are to be
truly fulfilled:

> At the beginning God expressed himself. That personal expres-
> sion, that word, was with God and was God, and he existed with
> God from the beginning. All creation took place through him,
> and none took place without him. In him appeared life and
> this life was the light of mankind. The light still shines in the
> darkness, and the darkness has never put it out (John 1:1–5,
> PHILLIPS).

Our selves, our souls, our whole identities are so tied up in
the person of Jesus Christ that attempting to discover or fulfill
anything in ourselves apart from Him means going at cross
purposes with our most basic beings. It is like trying to assemble some extremely complex machine without consulting the
directions or trying to unlock the mysteries of the Bible without
learning to read.

We were designed to "live and move and have our being" in
Christ (Acts 17:28). And we were created to function as contain-
ers for His being (2 Cor. 4:7). This is the foundational fact over
which we cannot leapfrog in our quest for understanding or
fulfillment. For apart from this basic reality, our lives at some
point will surely fall to pieces.

AN INNER FOCUS

"But," you interrupt (and rightly so), "if the whole answer is
surrendering to Jesus, why are there so many Christians whose
lives are falling to pieces in little and big ways?"

Sadly, I think this happens when we allow the myriad complications of our lives to pull our inner focus off Jesus.

Once Jesus called Peter to come to Him by walking on top of the
water (Matt. 14:28–31). Peter was able to do that only so long as he
kept his eyes focused on Jesus. It was as though the molecules of
the water held together and made a solid path for Peter's feet so
long as his gaze was upon the Lord. But once his eyes dropped
down to focus on the water, the path gave way, broke apart, dis-
solving into its liquid state, and Peter began to sink.

Now I'm sure that Peter, being a fisherman, was well aware of the "impossibility" of what Jesus was asking Him to do. He knew that people cannot walk on water. And yet because of his overwhelming faith in Jesus, Peter was willing and able to suspend his belief in the basic properties of liquid in favor of a higher belief.

I believe this story is a wonderful metaphor for the Christian walk. Jesus calls every child of His to come to Him, walking on the water of life's complications. He calls every one of us, His followers, to voluntarily suspend our belief in the discouraging "facts" of our situations and to believe instead in His overcoming life and power. When we keep our inner gaze, the eyes of our spirits, focused on Christ, the complexities and complications hold together in Him and make a solid path for our feet.

The Bible assures us that Jesus is very much in touch with the realities of our daily struggles and frustrations. He knows all about living day to day in this fragmented world—He did it! ("For we have no superhuman High Priest to whom our weaknesses are unintelligible—he himself has shared fully in all our experience . . . " Heb. 4:15, PHILLIPS.) Nor is God the Father unaware of our needs; He understands them even better than we do. ("Your Heavenly Father knows [all you need]," Matt. 6:32.)

It is with a full and compassionate comprehension of our human predicament that God calls us to turn our eyes on Him. And it is His promise that if we look first to Him, He will take care of whatever else we're worried about (see Matt. 6:33). "Change your focus," He seems to be saying. "Look at Me, just look at Me, and you'll be surprised at how those pieces of your life will begin to pull together into a meaningful whole."

Spike's cousin Kym once sent me a therapeutic little paperback book in much the same way that a lifeguard might throw a life preserver to a drowning man. Out into the deeps of overcommitment and daily desperation where she could see me floundering, she tossed me a copy of Carole Mayhall's *Lord of My Rocking Boat*.

In the book, Mayhall recalls battling the raging storm of her own life's confusion and complexity. Above the roar of the storm, she heard the words of Jesus speaking directly to her: "Carole, stop looking at the waves. Turn around and look at Me."

And as her vision narrowed to His life and purposes alone, she discovered in prayer the real key to the simplicity she had been seeking for so long. She writes:

Lord
Show me how to simplify.
Life is so complex,
The ministry so multiple,
Problems so monumental
I get a handle on one,
Only to have three more
Thrust upon me.
I feel so overwhelmed, Lord.

Please, simplify my life.
He said
Dear child, remember the words,
"This *one* thing I do.
I press toward the mark
Of the high calling of God."
My calling is simple.
It is this.
Obey me.[1]

In our Wednesday morning Bible study, we sing a lovely little chorus called "Turn Your Eyes upon Jesus." Most of us come there on Wednesdays from a variety of household and/or career stresses. But as we begin to sing, we can feel an actual ebbing of the stress level in the room. As we turn our spirit-eyes to Him, the focus of our hearts is gently shifted as well.

Scripture tells us to "seek the Lord and His strength: Seek His face continually" (1 Chron. 16:11). "Mine eyes are continually toward the Lord," says the psalmist, "for He will pluck my feet out of the net" (Ps. 25:15). When a hundred demands are pulling at us like unruly children or tearing at us like wild animals, we are invited to turn our eyes upon Jesus, "seeking His face." And as we do, the confusion seems to clear. We are able to see that we need not do a hundred things; we need only do one—obey Him, one small task at a time. Then suddenly we find the flower of peace blooming in a field of frustration. We find the gentle flow of order springing up in a desert of chaos.

What happens when we turn our eyes upon Jesus? How does He work? Exactly what gets transformed when we choose to focus our hearts and lives on Him? I can share with you three specific ways that the Lord works in my own life when I turn my eyes on Him—ways that cause me to feel less fragmented: (1) He gathers

the "pieces" of my situation and begins to work with what I *have*
until it becomes what I *need*, (2) He gives me eyes to see the beauty
and value in other people, and (3) He teaches me to focus on the
pieces of my life one person and one moment at a time.

Fragment Gathering

Gathering up my "pieces" is the first thing I observe the Lord
doing in my own life when I turn my eyes upon Him. I am
encouraged to see in Scripture that our God is in the business of
gathering up pieces. He has been doing this for a long time:

> On a certain hillside,
> on a certain afternoon,
> Jesus told the wonders of the kingdom
> 'til the day had slipped away.
> The hour was late;
> the people were hungry;
> the food was scarce.
> "What have we to work with?"
> was His only question
> (as it still is today).
> Giving thanks,
> He gathered the pieces
> of a little boy's lunch
> to feed a multitude
> (as He does today).
>
> In a time of darkness,
> in a burst of light,
> Jesus came to bring a kingdom of hope
> to a hopeless people.
> Their souls were lost;
> their needs were great;
> their resources seemed scarce.
> "What have we to work with?"
> was His only question
> (as it is today).
> Giving thanks,
> He gathered a harvest
> of fishermen and harlots,
> tax collectors, lepers,

and other sorts of losers
and made a church
to lead a lost creation
(as He does today).[2]

How many times in different ways has the Lord said simply, "Yield up the pieces, the scraps, the leftovers of your lives. All you've got is all I need to make a mountain from your molehill of faith"?

He said that through Elisha to a woman who came to the prophet in great distress. Her sons were about to be sold into slavery as a settlement for her late husband's debts.

"What have we to work with?" Elisha asked. The widow had one small container of oil—nothing else of value.

"Gather up all of your empty vessels—whatever old pots and pitchers you can find or borrow," the prophet commended, "and begin to fill them with oil."

The widow did as she was bid, and she found to her amazement that there was enough oil to fill every vessel—enough to pay the debt and keep her family for life (2 Kings 4:1–7).

At a wedding feast in Cana, the party was lengthy, the crowd was thirsty, and the wine ran out. "What have we to work with?" our Lord asked again. The vessels were gathered and filled, the thanks was given, the party was saved (John 2:1–10).

Can you see the principle operating in these stories—a principle that also operates in our lives? Pieces and leftovers that seem to amount to little or nothing, once yielded thankfully to Him, can become much. Empty and useless vessels, when placed in His hands, are filled.

Our Lord stands ready to transform all that we offer (when it is all that we have) into all that we need. He waits eagerly to pour out a love, a mercy, a transforming tenderness so powerful that what seems to us a jumble of disjointed pieces comes together in Him, forming a vessel of glory for Him to fill with the oil of healing and the sparkling wine of His joy.

In my own life, the most powerful example of the Lord's gathering my surrendered "pieces" and transforming them into what I needed is the way He led me into the songwriting profession. I had spent many restless years searching (though somewhat aimlessly at times) for something to do with my life. I had a strong feeling that if I could find the right "work" I would at last be happy.

It was during this period that I enrolled in a ten-day seminar called "Career Development," which was designed to help each person zero in on her best career area. As challenging as the seminar was to me, I also found it very frustrating, because I discovered through the tests we were given that I was good at a lot of things, but not really great at anything. And most of the talents and strengths I was able to unearth in myself seemed to be of the unmarketable variety.

I remember one woman in the seminar who looked up from the results of her "interests and abilities" test and muttered, "Oh great, I can either be a cheerleader or a yard man!" I felt sort of the same way. My experience performing in local musicals, my poetry writing, my degree in education (which I had no interest in pursuing), my memorized log of hundreds of songs from the thirties and forties that I learned at my father's knee, my ability to create crazy skits and sentimental songs for the birthdays and anniversaries of friends—what did it all add up to?

I wouldn't know the answer to that until much later. Once I had put the reins of my life into the hands of God, He took me out of the "career search" long enough for me to begin to get to know Him and His word. I found I had an insatiable desire to find out everything the Bible said about everything. For two uninterrupted years I studied hungrily with Betsy and Emilie, two friends who "took me to raise" as a baby Christian.

Interestingly, it was out of these Friday Bible studies, when I wasn't searching for anything at all, that a new career direction began to emerge. Little songs of praise would come to me as I studied; I wrote these down and shared them only in the privacy of our small group at first. Soon I was also writing love songs and patriotic songs and children's songs and anything else that came to mind. It was as though the words and music were pouring out of me!

As Spike shared the excitement of what I was doing, he became more and more convinced that I should seriously pursue my newly kindled interest in songwriting. He went out and bought me a tape recorder and bequeathed to me his old electric typewriter. At Christmas that year, he and the children helped me fix up a spare bedroom for an office of my own, and I was in business!

Spike's idea was that we would give my songwriting two years. If during that time I had no encouragement of any kind, we would

rethink our decision and try something else. But for the time being
he urged me to "go for it" with all of my energy and enjoyment,
and we'd see what happened. (I look back on that encouragement
from Spike as one of the most Christlike gifts I have ever received.
He believed in me completely from the beginning, regardless of
whether I was to become a brilliant success or a total failure. And I
know that by his very act of giving me permission to fail, he was
granting me the courage to succeed!)

Many exciting things came about as a result of this decision of
ours. The Lord added to my life teachers and mentors, co-writers
and publishers, as well as many encouraging friends without
whom I could not have succeeded. Many people told me that I
could never make it in the music industry without moving to
Nashville or Los Angeles, but the Lord just closed my ears to that
kind of talk. And gently His Holy Spirit kept nudging me through
each successive door that was opened before me.

When I had accumulated a tiny catalogue of compositions,
Spike began urging me to take my first trip to Nashville. And so,
with a plastic file of lyrics and tapes in tow, Betsy and I headed out
into the icy January of 1978 for my first Music Row experience.

What an adventure! Because of the weather (one of the biggest
snowstorms of the year) I was only able to make and keep ap-
pointments with a few people. In fact, Interstate 65 was closed
for five days, and we spent that time sitting in the guest bedroom
of Betsy's friends, the Wolfes, totally "snowed in." But it was a
beginning. It was through those early trips to Nashville and my
newly acquired associates there that I was able to get my songs
and lyrics before some people who could help me.

Well within the two-year trial period that we had established,
my first song was recorded—a ballad entitled "You Gave Me Love
When Nobody Gave Me a Prayer" (co-written with Archie Jor-
dan). What a thrill to see those simple lines I had scribbled on the
back of an envelope go on to become the title song on the 1979
Grammy-award winning album of B. J. Thomas! Many other
recordings were to follow.

In Ephesians, Paul writes that Jesus is able to accomplish in us
"infinitely more than we ever dare to ask or imagine" (Eph. 3:20,
PHILLIPS). I had dreamed of an exciting and fulfilling career, but
the Lord had even better dreams in store! In His perfect season,
He gathered up the fragments of my life and led me a step at
a time, walking on the water, to a better place—one that I

couldn't even have dreamed up in my imagination to ask Him for. There He put together a career that seems almost tailor-made for me.

One of the most exciting things to me about the Lord's "fragment gathering" in my own life has been to look back and see that He didn't waste a thing. My experience in stage musicals has been invaluable in creating choir musicals for the church. My knowledge of hundreds of old pop songs by great writers such as George and Ira Gershwin, Rodgers and Hammerstein, and others was as good as a college degree in lyric writing. My actual degree in education has even been put to good use in the teaching of songwriting seminars to aspiring new writers.

A New Perspective

A second change that takes place in us as we focus our hearts and lives on the Lord is that He begins to give us a new way to look at the people in our lives. It is as though our whole value system starts to shift inside us, like the pieces of broken glass in the kaleidoscope, and we become able to see new levels of beauty and value beneath the surface in other people.

Jesus looked at people this way. On the exterior, Peter appeared to be an impulsive, outspoken fisherman with a rash temper and a hasty tongue. But Jesus saw something else. Jesus saw the potential for a strong and loyal kingdom leader, and He called Peter "the rock."

The people of her village saw the woman at the well as a person of loose morals and low esteem. Jesus looked beyond these things to the motivation behind her lifestyle. He saw the spiritual thirst within her, and He promised her living water that would quench that thirst for eternity.

When I think of a person who sees people this way—looking beyond the exterior to the beauty and value within—I always think of our friend Norman Grubb, the elderly author-evangelist. I will never forget Norman's first visit to our home. We had agreed to house him while he was in Mobile for a speaking engagement. Norman walked into our family knowing nothing about us at all. We served him tea (he's English) and sat for a time in our den visiting and enjoying the colorful variety of birds landing on the feeder just outside the window.

With a twinkle in his blue eyes, Norman turned to Spike, whom he had only just met, and said, "Spike, I see the Father in you!" Spike was frankly surprised. (What Norman didn't know was that, although Spike was a believer, he had been away from church for a number of years. I hardly think Spike had anticipated this kind of affirmation from a "religious leader.")

"Anyone who feeds and cares for the little birds as you do," Norman continued, "must be very like his Heavenly Father." The Christ in Norman had connected with the beautiful, valuable qualities in Spike and affirmed them.

When we see the beauty and value in each person we meet as Norman does—as Jesus did—then every moment that we are with that person will be beautiful and valuable as well. Mother Teresa has said many times that she finds the face of Jesus in the face of every person she cares for, and this is what brings joy and glory to her work.

One Thing at a Time

The third change that begins to occur in us when we center our lives on Jesus is that we experience a heightened capacity to focus our attention on one person, one task, one event at a time, as He did. When Jesus moved through the crowded village streets, the needs of the people pressed in all around Him. But it was as though He had an internal filtering system which would push back the clamor of the many in order for Him to listen for the quiet heart cry of the one. Compassionately, deliberately, He was able to hear and meet one need at a time and then move on.

It's interesting to note that Jesus was able to stop and focus totally on the needs of others in spite of the fact that His Life was on a specific course, moving toward a specific goal. He was not aimlessly wandering through the countryside, as it may have seemed to some, but actually moving toward the most important destiny any man will ever have. He knew the ultimate call on His life (Heb. 12:2). His face was set toward Jerusalem (Luke 9:51). And yet Jesus was able to treat the "interruptions" along the way as what they actually were—a part of His purpose.

Even at the Last Supper, when the Lord's mind must certainly have been consumed with thoughts of what lay ahead for Him, He was able to set those concerns aside for the evening. With focused love and care, He was then able to use the time for ministry to His disciples—teaching, comforting, sharing with, and serving them to the end.

It was this kind of present-moment, focused living that the Lord made possible for Spike and me as we drove up into the Smokey Mountains a short while back. It was Parents' Weekend at the University of the South in Sewanee, Tennessee, where our son Curt is enrolled as a freshman. The mountains were ablaze with autumn leaves, and the beautiful Cambridge-like campus was decorated at every turn with the changing colors of the season.

What an incredible time we had! We met Curt's teachers and friends and got from him a complete guided tour of his new domain. Saturday night, crowded into the local pizza hangout with tables and tables of other families, we had a leisurely and memorable visit with our son.

"I just want to say thanks for everything you've done for me, Mom and Dad, and I love you," he said matter-of-factly between bites. Huge tears splashed off my chin into the pizza sauce. It was a peak moment.

All in all, I look back on that weekend as a topaz-colored jewel that I will cherish all my life. Really. It was that terrific. But here's the real miracle of it: Spike and I were able to thoroughly enjoy every moment of the weekend, even knowing that we were heading back to Mobile on Monday to face a week that included (1) an IRS audit, and (2) my hysterectomy! The Lord allowed both of us to set aside our concerns over those things in order to seize that special opportunity for joy that He had provided.

Focusing on one moment at a time includes not only seizing and savoring the peak moments like that wonderful weekend, but also accepting and embracing the "dailiness," with its routines and intrusions. (Our friends Tom and Mimi call this "the art of taking life in small bites.")

THE PIECES ARE THE WHOLE

Henri Nouwen, in his book *Out of Solitude*, tells of an old Notre Dame professor who had always complained that his work was constantly being interrupted. Like so many of us, he longed for the freedom to concentrate fully on what he considered

important. Late in his life, however, the professor came to realize
that the interruptions *were* his work.

This is the "conversion" of our hearts, says Nouwen—"to recognize and believe that the many unexpected events are not just
disturbing interruptions of our projects, but the way in which
God molds our hearts."[3]

Or as Anne Ortlund puts it, "God, who loves you very much,
has tailor-made all your . . . circumstances, your relationships
—to pressure you into becoming that beautiful [person] He's
planned for you to be."[4] Once He gives us eyes to see His hand in
the seeming randomness of our daily circumstances, He also
begins to give us a desire and ability to live according to His
agenda and not our own.

The interruptions *are* the work. The pieces *are* the whole. We
cannot wait for a total, personal revelation of all that God has for
us to be handed down in one lump sum. God reveals Himself
to us bit by spiritual bit. Even our broadest visions and our
highest goals, once we know them, must be broken down and
lived out in the small particulars of our everyday lives, if they are
to have meaning.

"The goal and the way cannot long endure in separation," says
Abraham Heschel in his book, *Man's Quest for God.* "The days of
the week, the food we eat, the holidays of the year, the deeds we
do—these are the frontiers of faith."[5] When I am learning to
value the small, disjointed events in my day, learning to "sense
the holy that is available in the everyday," as Heschel put it, then
I begin to discern that these scraps of significance are cells in the
body of my life's meaning.

Once the hand of God set Ezekiel down in the middle of a
valley of dry bones. "Lo, they were *very* dry," said Ezekiel.

But the Lord said to the bones, "I will cause breath to enter
you that you may come to life. And I will put sinews on you,
make flesh grow back on you, cover you with skin, and put
breath in you that you may come alive; and you will know that I
am the Lord."

And as soon as Ezekiel spoke the words the Lord told him to
speak, "behold, a rattling[!]; and the bones came together, bone
to its bone" (Ezek. 37:1–7, emphasis mine).

When our lives are feeling to us as dry and disconnected as
Ezekiel's bones, the Lord our God stands ready and waiting to

gather the pieces and breathe into our dryness the breath of His incredible new life. As we center our hearts on Him, He begins to give us eyes to see the beauty in others, the blessing hidden in the small disjointed moment, and the ability to stop and focus on each. He longs to assemble the parts and pieces of who we are into lives of wholeness and continuity that only He can create.

FATHER, WE THANK YOU for Jesus Your Son, the One in whom all things hold together. Help us to center our hearts and our minds on Him. And give us the grace to make peace with the pieces of our lives, knowing that You are continually drawing them together into a meaningful whole according to Your purpose. In Jesus' name we pray. AMEN.

P.S. O Lord, how presumptuous I am to think that I can wrap this chapter up and tie it with a nice, neat bow. Things are not that simple. I don't have all the answers. I mean, I talk a good game, but I have to confess to You how far I am from being able to live the things I write.

Here I was this morning, so driven and compulsive about finishing the "important" task at hand (this chapter) that I totally forgot to do the very thing I've been writing about. I was so busy following my own selfish little agenda that I ignored Your agenda and stood up my sweet friend Jacque, who really needed my friendship today.

Lord, I'm such a jerk. It's so tempting for me to give up on myself. And yet You never give up on me. Heal me, Lord. Forgive my selfishness, and reconcile me to my friend. Teach me to see Your hand in the disjointed pieces of today and to know that the interruptions are the work! AMEN AGAIN.

Celebrate the Temporary

(Chorus)
Celebrate the temporary, celebrate the now,
Celebrate the temporary, love will show you how!
Lift your heart to God who's great,
Do not wait, don't hesitate,
Now's the time to celebrate—celebrate it now!

Here today and gone tomorrow,
Time is only ours to borrow
All the joy and all the sorrow—celebrate Him now!
Celebrate the Love that found us;
He has cut the chains that bound us.
Free to love the world around us—celebrate Him now!

(Repeat Chorus)

We can't see beyond the minute,
If you've got a dream, begin it,
He will put His Spirit in it—celebrate Him now!
Celebrate the One who sees us,
Celebrate the Love that frees us,
Lifting up the name of Jesus—celebrate Him now!

(Repeat Chorus)

Like the bits of glass in the kaleidoscope, our lives are broken.

Broken Vessels, Healing Hands 4
A Redemptive View of Suffering

THE MAIN SANCTUARY of our church, which was built in 1823, is lined on both sides by huge, old, exquisitely detailed stained-glass windows. Added to the church one or two at a time over the years, the windows depict scenes and characters from the Bible. (Two of the most impressive ones were designed by the internationally renowned artist, Louis Comfort Tiffany.) Almost every week, a number of tourists are drawn to the church by its historical markers and are given a tour by our hospitable caretaker, Gilbert Brantley.

But our church building is not a museum for relics. It stands not to commemorate a list of long-deceased, stained-glass saints, but to open its doors to live ones. It is very much in the business of the here and now, for it houses a living body, the body of Jesus Christ. On its well-worn pews sit the flesh-and-blood, struggle-and-tears, real-life people who make up His living body on this earth today.

One Sunday not long ago, I sat near the back of the church watching the early sunshine come through those old windows. As the light poured its color over the heads and shoulders of the congregation, I was struck by my growing love for this interesting assortment of people. And as my eyes moved from friend to friend, I saw in a new light something I had observed before but had never really put into words: the presence of pain in so many of their lives.

Here was a family grieving over the loss of a son, a wife just recovering from a miscarriage, a father out of work, a young woman in her thirties who would love to be married but who lives alone, another woman still trying to accept the divorce that has split her twenty-five-year marriage. Up and down the rows my eyes traveled. Almost every family was dealing with some kind of personal struggle.

"Lord," I prayed, "what is going on? There are so many of us hurting. I don't remember its being like this a few years ago. Lord, are people hurting more these days?"

"No," His silent answer came to my heart. "It's just that you are caring more these days."

THE PROBLEM OF PAIN

The world is full of pain. And the simple truth which struck me so forcefully that day is this: the church is full of pain, too! To be a member of Christ's Body, living in any kind of honest fellowship within a church family, is to be in constant, close contact with the brokenness that is a part of the human condition. It's not only all around us—it's within us.

Suffering is one of the most difficult and baffling subjects with which we Christians have to contend. But contend with it me must, and I have a hunch that until we've wrestled it down to a place of personal understanding and acceptance, any spiritual progress we make is going to be "slow-goin'."

Psychiatrist Viktor Frankl, who survived the horror of the German concentration camps of World War II, wrote this about suffering:

> To live is to suffer, to survive is to find meaning in the suffering. If there is a purpose in life at all, there must be a purpose in suffering and dying. But no man can tell another what this purpose is. Each must find out for himself, and must accept the responsibility that his answer prescribes. If he succeeds, he will continue to grow in spite of all indignities.[1]

I certainly don't presume to know all of the answers to man's questions about suffering. Comparatively speaking, I have not suffered all that much. And I don't pretend to know what you are needing on your journey toward wholeness. But I do believe the words of my friend Virginia, who loved me through some pain of my own.

"Claire," she said, "if we are here for anything, it's to help each other through. If you can't understand it all right now, that's okay. Grab on to my faith—it's big enough to keep both of us afloat!" And it was!

So I lovingly lay out before you some simple conclusions I have come to on my own journey. I hope that exploring these insights may help you if you or someone you love is hurting. But if they don't exactly seem to fit where you are, that's okay, too. Try to hang on anyway.

Healing is a process. Someday you may look back at something I have said, and it may fit you like a glove. And someday something *you* know and share may be the very thing *I* need to make it through. There is nothing more certain on this Christian walk than our desperate need for one another.

LIFE IS TROUBLES

Have you ever heard a sermon that reminded you of the sales pitch of a traveling medicine salesman? "Just one teaspoon of this, little lady, and you'll be rid of every problem you've ever had, from your headaches to your hangnails. Step right up!" There's a lot of that kind of sermonizing going around these days—the kind about the trouble-free existence we are "gar-on-teed" once we join up with Jesus.

Well it just ain't so, and nobody in the Bible ever said it was—least of all Jesus! The first conclusion I have made is that *suffering is inevitable, even for Christians.* Every life will include its share of trials and troubles.

I'll never forget where I was when I saw my first copy of M. Scott Peck's *The Road Less Traveled.*[2] My friend Carolyn and I were thumbing through the newly released volumes at our favorite neighborhood bookstore. I read the first line in Peck's book and held it under Carolyn's nose for her inspection. She read it, our eyes met, and simultaneously our heads began to nod in agreement. That famous first line: "Life is difficult."

Trying to go at life from any other basic premise is asking for extra trouble. An understanding of life as a series of difficult challenges is realistic, *not* pessimistic, and the sooner we make peace with this reality, the better.

John DeFrain, in his book *Secrets of Strong Families,* reminisces about his grandmother Effie's deathbed wisdom. After listening to her middle-aged son Orville describe his current troubles in detail, the old woman nodded patiently and said solemnly, "Life *is* troubles."[3]

"Man is born for trouble as sparks fly upward," says the Book of Job (5:7). In 1 Thessalonians, Paul writes, "But of course you know that such troubles are a part of God's plan for us Christians" (3:3, LB). And in John 16:33, we get it straight from the Savior's mouth: "In the world you *will* have tribulation: but be of good cheer, I have overcome the world!" (NKJV, emphasis mine). The Lord is warning us of the bumps ahead. But all the while He is assuring us that He'll be with us on the journey to make sure we reach our destination!

Given the facts of daily life, it is surprising how many people are still resistant to this idea of inevitable suffering. Perhaps in the United States, a cultural conspiracy of Walt Disney, the American Dream, and the Hollywood Ending is responsible for the popular notion that we human beings are somehow "entitled" to a happy and trouble-free life.

But people who choose to spread out this "entitlement theory" as their blanket for life's picnic are in for some additional grief. Not only will they suffer their own quotient of discouragement and difficulty; they will also suffer the disillusionment of not getting what they felt entitled to!

Henri Nouwen, in his excellent book *The Wounded Healer,* contends that suffering can only be dealt with constructively when we learn to view it as part of life's package—as "integral to the human condition." Once we have begun to accept this brokenness in our lives and share it with each other, we become free to "mobilize" our shared suffering into "a common search for life."[4]

A QUESTION OF FAITH

At some time or another almost everyone struggles with the question of suffering—why people must go through it, where it comes from, and what it's all about. I have asked these questions myself and have concluded that there are no pat, easy answers to them. We can definitely receive insight from studying God's Word and from prayer. But at some point for every Christian, *dealing with the questions surrounding suffering will become an exercise of faith.*

My own wrestling with this issue of suffering and brokenness began when my two-year-old niece, Jenny deGravelles, was tragically killed in an automobile accident in 1977. I was heartbroken for my brother, Johnny, and his wife, Jan, yet I felt totally helpless in my efforts to comfort them. I felt that as a Christian I should have the answers, yet nothing I knew seemed able to touch the amount of pain they were experiencing. All I could do was write them little love letters and cling to my knowledge of God as a loving Father. I trusted Him, though I did not understand.

Then several years later, I walked with a friend through a similar tragedy which reactivated all of my earlier questions. Little Katie, the infant daughter of our dear friends and next-door neighbors, Bob and Katherine Zarzour, died following heart surgery.

I remember the day of her death as though it were yesterday. Katie had made it through a complex and lengthy surgery in Birmingham. Everyone was elated—and then her little heart just stopped. Impossible. Impossible that she should die with all of our prayers so strongly behind her. (I believe that if there is an "intercession-meter" in heaven, it probably blew a fuse the day of Katie's operation! Every prayer group we knew of in about five states had been working overtime praying for Katie.)

I must have walked ten miles that afternoon. I had this feeling that somebody had let us down, and all the arrows of doubt were pointing to heaven.

"Why?" I kept asking over and over almost involuntarily. "Why, why, why?"

After many miles of walking, something unusual happened. Weary and far from home, I was walking past a string of beautiful suburban yards and patios that faced onto the street. One patio was decorated for a party, and music was blaring over a sound system.

I had heard the song that was playing hundreds of times, but I had never really focused on the words. Suddenly I was hearing them as though they were brand new. The song was the old pop hit, "Let It Be." It filled my ears and echoed through my consciousness with what I felt somehow was a message for me, though I did not understand it then. The voice over the sound system was assuring me that *there would be an answer* someday, and encouraging me to "let it be."

The weeks and months that followed were incredibly painful

for my friend Katherine, Katie's mom. I tried to be there for her, to listen and care. But many days I felt helpless and empty-handed. There seemed to be no way to give her a transfusion of the hope I knew was valid—no way to translate my truth into a language that her broken heart could hear. I could see her pain, but I couldn't help. How I ached for her! And the question "why" was never far from my mind.

In the years since Katie's death, I have continued to ask the Lord for understanding. And though He has not given me that one all-encompassing theological answer, He has taught me some valuable lessons about the connection between faith and suffering.

God Is in Control

Many Christians are reluctant to acknowledge any connection between God and suffering. Some see Satan as the only cause for the hard times we all go through. Others blame every difficulty in this life on the fact that we are members of a fallen creation whose rebellion has inflicted suffering on the world.

I believe that these views are interrelated, and that both are true. Satan does cause suffering. Scripture describes him as a thief, a liar, and a destroyer, and we are encouraged to learn to do battle with him, wearing the whole armor of God (see Eph. 6:10–18).

It is also true that tremendous suffering has resulted from humankind's choice to follow Satan into rebellion against God's way. The world is reaping the *natural consequences* of man's fallen condition—in the wars that rage among nations, in the breakdown of the family, in the appalling spread of sexually transmitted diseases.

But I believe it is important for us Christians to know that regardless of where suffering originates, God is now, has always been, and always will be in control of His universe. Satan has not "pulled any fast ones" on the King of kings and Lord of lords. Sinful mankind has not managed to foil heaven's best intentions while some powerless diety was catching a catnap! God is sovereign! He is God! Whatever happens in His universe has happened with God's knowledge and permission. And this includes suffering.

We may never understand fully in this life why some things occur. "For now we see in a mirror, dimly, but then face to face; now I know in part, but then I shall know fully just as I also have been fully known" (1 Cor. 13:12). Until we know fully, we must exercise faith. Where understanding is partial, faith must fill in the blanks. For if we choose to "move on" as Christians, I believe it is vital that we acknowledge our God in every kind of situation, good or evil. To become ambivalent on this subject of God's sovereignty is to become paralyzed on our spiritual journeys.

Morris Townsend, husband of my late friend Josephine, often told the story of what he called his "furnace experience." Morris's very successful career in finance (which included a term as National Director of the United States Treasury) was cut short by a series of unforeseen events. In a matter of weeks, he was divested of fortune, position, and reputation. Morris said that through this experience he learned to see and actively recognize God at work in even the most devastating events. Like Joseph in the Old Testament, who was stripped of money, family, and honor, Morris learned to see the loving, sovereign hand of God at work in his circumstances. He learned to say, as Joseph did, "You meant evil against me, but God meant it for good" (Gen. 50:20).[5]

Suffering Makes Us Christlike

How does suffering figure into our lives as disciples of Jesus? Clearly, we Christians are not exempt from suffering. And though He does not provide us with a complete outline of His reasons, I believe the Lord intends for us to walk through some difficult times on the way to His kingdom. As Brennan Manning points out in his book *Lion and Lamb,*

> Jesus never explained the "why" of suffering. . . . He simply made it the indispensable condition for discipleship. . . . Never once did He attempt to charm anyone to His service with fair promises of happiness. On the contrary, with uncompromising honesty, He said, "If anyone will come after me, let him take up his cross daily."[6]

The specifics of "taking up our cross" may vary. Whenever asked about the price of discipleship, for instance, Jesus was quick to mention homelessness (Luke 9:58), sacrifice (Luke 18:18–23), and estrangement from family (Matt. 10:34), among others. But whatever form our suffering takes, we are promised that in God's hands it can have a positive purpose.

As John Wimber puts it, "regardless of the *immediate* reasons for the suffering, the *ultimate* reason is . . . that we might become like Jesus."[7] Scripture makes it clear that God the Father is molding us into the image of His Son (Rom. 8:29). How can we ever expect to resemble the "Man of Sorrows" without having experienced real sorrow? God can use every heartache and difficulty to make us like Jesus.

Suffering Requires a Faith Surrender

But in order to be molded by our sorrows, we must choose to be "moldable." Being moldable means becoming yielded clay in the Potter's hands. How do we achieve this moldability? I believe it is best achieved by surrendering to Him whatever pain, anger, or unresolved questions have resulted from our suffering, trusting Him to use them for His purposes in our lives.

This type of surrender is definitely a step of faith. If all pain were removed and all questions answered, faith would not be the central requirement of our Christian commitment. But it is.

One of the most difficult things about coming to this kind of faith-surrender of our anger and questioning is the very human problem of comparisons. It would be so much easier to accept and deal with our quotient of "tribulation" if we weren't constantly comparing ours to somebody else's—or comparing Friend A's ordeal with Friend B's life of ease and declaring it an injustice.

I'm from a big family of competitive siblings. Growing up, we must have driven our parents wild with our constant insistence that everything be kept "fair": "He had three cookies, so I should have three." "I never got to stay out 'til midnight when I was her age!"

Many of us tend to keep up this reasoning on a spiritual level with our heavenly Parent. We tend to think that we, with our finite minds, know what is just, and we try to impose our notion of justice on God.

But Jesus never promises that things in our lives will work out according to our specifications or designs when we choose to follow Him. When He calls us to Himself, He asks for a complete exchange. He asks for all of us, in exchange for all of Himself, without handing out any guarantees about life's "fairness." He calls us to run the race, keeping our eyes on the goal, looking neither to the left nor to the right (Heb. 12:1). I believe one reason He does this is to keep us from comparing our "race" to someone else's.

After the Resurrection, Jesus appeared to the disciples at the Sea of Tiberias. There He was able to give them some last-minute teaching before He ascended to His Father (John 21:20–23). Some of the disciples had heard rumors that John was somehow going to be exempt from physical death, and Peter (who was busy comparing his own "race" with John's) was anxious to get the straight story from Jesus.

"Lord, what about this man?" he asked. ("If You let him stay alive, You should let me, too," I can almost hear Peter saying.)

But Jesus cuts Peter short with this very telling statement: "If I want him to remain until I come, what is that to you? You follow me!" ("What I do or decide or permit or forbid in the life of another person is none of your concern," He seems to be saying to us. "Your concern is to walk with Me. I, who love you tenderly, will make decisions regarding your life. Stop comparing and follow Me.")

God Deals with Us Individually

Comparisons are not valid in the Christian walk because God works with each of us individually, one heart at a time. If we remain open to Him during times of suffering, He will bring each of us into a place of acceptance of our own pain, creating a way that is *uniquely right for us.* It may be a victory or an escape. It may be a time for spiritual warfare, for healing, for resting, for waiting, or for learning. It may even be a new avenue for ministry. He does not solve every problem with the same solution— and His timetable is definitely His own.

This means that none of us can tell anyone else how to react to suffering. For me to rush into your situation and try to tell you how to interpret your suffering or how to process your grief could be worse than useless. It could be very harmful, for it could work against the very thing that God is trying to do in your life. (I'm thankful now that my little love letters to Jan and Johnny were not loaded with all the "right answers" on how to grieve. I'm thankful, too, that I didn't know *what* to say to Katherine, because "advice" was not really required!)

Our friend Laura Barr, who is a wonderful speaker and Bible teacher, strongly stresses this point when she lectures on suffering and grief. She tells how at age thirteen, after her father's sudden and unexpected death, she was told by a well-meaning friend of the family, "There, there. God needed your Daddy in heaven more than we do on earth." Laura says she looked around at her widowed mother, who was left alone to raise five children, and could only conclude, "What did God need with my Daddy? God owns everything and everybody. But I only had one Daddy. What kind of loving God is He?" Because of the damage done to her by this well-intended remark, Laura frequently cautions fellow Christians not to force-feed their own personal spiritual answers to others in grief.

But if we shouldn't give our personal answers to a friend who is suffering or grieving, just exactly what advice should we offer? To that I would answer, "as little as possible." A simple "I love you" or "I'm so sorry" or "I'm hurting with you" are usually more than enough. And sometimes just silently "being there" speaks the loudest of all.

Our friends Lucy and Billy Lyons have appreciated this "being there" kind of sympathy so much since the death last summer of their thirteen-year-old son, Radcliff. One incident particularly comes to mind.

The day of Radcliff's funeral, Billy turned around and found himself looking into the tear-filled eyes of a friend he had not seen in years—a man with whom he had played college football at the University of Southern Mississippi.

"I don't know a single thing to say, Billy. All I can do is cry with you," he said. The two friends hugged one another, then settled down on the sofa and wept wordlessly together for a long, long time. Billy told me that of all the well-meaning things people tried to tell him about Radcliff, nothing spoke louder to him than the tears of his friend.

It is so important to remember that God is dealing with each hurting person individually. We don't need to instruct each other in how to suffer. The type and duration of grief that each of us follows cannot be forced or imitated. It must take its own path if we are to grow through and out of suffering.

A Personal Note

A long time after little Katie's death, I began gradually to be able to apply faith to some of my own questions and release them. I gave up my need to have all the right answers for the wounded ones that I love—that is God's department!

I read with new meaning the beautiful words of Isaiah 45. In this passage, I could clearly hear my God calling me to trust Him in all things. I could hear Him calling to all who have been broken, troubled, grief-stricken, or tormented by questions, to finally "let it be":

> I am the Lord, and there is no other;
> Besides Me there is no God. . . .
> I am the Lord, and there is no other,
> The One forming light and creating darkness,
> Causing well-being and creating calamity;
> I am the Lord who does all these. . . .
> Woe to the one who quarrels with his Maker—
> An earthenware vessel among the vessels of earth!
> Will the clay say to the potter, "What are you doing?" . . .
> You shall commit to Me the work of My hands.
> It is I who made the earth, and created man upon it. . . .
> A righteous God and a Savior. . . .
> Turn to Me, and be saved, all the ends of the earth;
> For I am God, and there is no other.
> I have sworn by Myself,
> The word has gone forth from My mouth in righteousness
> And will not turn back,
> That to Me every knee will bow, every tongue will
>   swear allegiance. . . . (vv. 5–23).

Something in that strong passage of Scripture touched me and spoke to me personally. I felt again with awe what a wondrous God I serve—"a righteous God and a savior," whose thoughts and ways are higher than my own (Isa. 55:8–10). I felt the nearness of the One who loved me enough to suffer and die in my place. And suddenly I was overwhelmed with a spiritual

weariness from all of my struggling to swim against the current
of His kingdom. That day I prayed,

> God, I love You. I choose to trust You. I believe You are a
> sovereign God. I don't understand why Katie did not live when
> we all prayed so hard, but I'm surrendering my questions now to
> You. Only You know and understand. I choose now to operate out
> of faith, Lord. I am surrendering my anger and frustration to You.
> I am surrendering my fear of losing one of my own children. If
> that day should come, Lord, You will be here to see me through.
>
> You are a God of love—I know that. You loved little Katie—
> You still do. You love Bob and Katherine, and I know that, in their
> suffering, You are suffering too.
>
> Someday we will understand. Someday "we will know even as
> we have been fully known." But for now, Lord, begin to heal my
> friends. Help them to move forward. Help them to return the
> broken pieces of their lives to You. Shine through their broken-
> ness, Lord, and create something beautiful from those pieces, for
> their good and Your glory.

By the grace of God I found the faith to pray that prayer of
surrender. And by His all-sufficient grace, I continue to surrender
to Him on a daily basis all of these same things—my anger and
questions and fears—for Him to heal and answer and relieve.

A GLORY IN SUFFERING

The third conclusion I have made about suffering is that *for the
child of God, there is glory in suffering.* Though it may not always
miraculously eradicate all pain, God's redemptive process goes
to work immediately in behalf of those who "love [Him] . . .
who are called according to His purpose" (Rom. 8:28). His presence is very near to us when we are hurting (Ps. 34:18; Matt.
5:4), for He is committed to moving the negative forces in our
lives toward positive ends. In fact, it is frequently the brokenness
in a heart or a situation that seems to open the door to the
redemptive power of God.

Paul Tournier, in his book *Creative Suffering,* says, "If anything is certain, it is that every one of life's trials, if only because it breaks the hard crust of our physical and mental habits,

creates, like the ploughing of a field, an empty space where a seed can be sown."[8]

In the lives of people who have suffered I find a depth of beauty and grace not present in the life untouched by trouble. (In terms of the kaleidoscope metaphor, it seems that the pieces of glass with the most broken edges are the ones which catch the most light!) And part of the glory of suffering comes in watching the Lord use the very circumstances of our brokenness to fashion new opportunities for blessing.

God's glory comes to His children in many different "packages" during times of tribulation. Here are four that I have observed and experienced: (a) character, (b) confidence, (c) comfort, and (d) compassion.

He Gives Us Character

Throughout Paul's Epistles, we find evidence of God's using trials to refine Paul's character. Paul even learned to "rejoice in [his] sufferings" because he found that "suffering produces endurance, and endurance produces character, and character produces hope" (Rom. 5:3–5). Through his "thorn in the flesh," Paul came to understand and glory in his weakness:

> In order to prevent my becoming absurdly conceited, I was given a physical handicap—one of Satan's angels—to harass me and effectually stop any conceit. Three times I begged the Lord for it to leave me, but his reply has been, "My grace is enough for you: for where there is weakness, my power is shown the more completely." Therefore, I have cheerfully made up my mind to be proud of my weaknesses, because they mean a deeper experience of the power of Christ. I can even enjoy weaknesses, suffering, privations, persecutions and difficulties for Christ's sake. For my very weakness makes me strong in him (2 Cor. 12:7–10, PHILLIPS).

Like Paul, I have often been thankful for the weakness and failure which led me to my night of decision for Christ. Like the psalmist, I have learned to say, "It is good for me that I was afflicted, that I might learn Thy statutes" (Ps. 119:71).

I came to Jesus that night emotionally and spiritually bankrupt. I had come face to face with my own sinfulness. I had no other "tricks up my sleeve." I had tried doing things my way, and I had found that without God my life was a flop. No wonder I can glory now in my weakness! Without it, I would never have found Jesus, who is my strength.

I recently heard someone compare our spiritual and emotional wounds to the great "wound" on the face of our land, the Grand Canyon. By studying the geological strata laid bare in the wall of the canyon, scientists have gained valuable information about the earth. In the same way, our times of brokenness provide us with valuable insight into the hidden layers of ourselves. This insight can in turn, by the power of God's Spirit, lead us to new levels of personal growth.

Paul E. Billheimer, in his book *Don't Waste Your Sorrows,* concludes that affliction "is the way God builds selfless character and develops *agape* love. Suffering, triumphantly accepted, slays the self-life, delivers one from self-centeredness, and frees one to love."[9]

He Gives Us Confidence

I love the little passage of Scripture which says, "In quietness and in confidence shall be our strength" (Isa. 30:15). It is often during trying times that the Lord pours out this kind of quiet confidence in our lives. A strength, a knowing, an ability to hold on in faith seems to take over in us, and we are able to make it through with tremendous grace.

Our dear friend Etta Edwards, who cleans our house on Mondays, recently went through a real time of testing. She was told by a doctor that she had a tumor in her breast which he feared was malignant. Etta said that the minute she heard his diagnosis, she could feel a quiet confidence growing in her spirit—a certainty that God meant to heal her.

With a boldness that is uncharacteristic of this gentle woman, she told the doctor, "I believe that the God who created me will heal me."

The doctor at this point informed Etta that God does not heal cancer. He also labeled her a "religious fanatic." Etta's soft but immediate response was, "If that means I'm crazy, well I guess you're right. I'm crazy for my Jesus!" She gathered her dignity about her like a cloak and left his office, never to return.

We found Etta another doctor who was kinder and more understanding, but equally certain that she was harboring a malignant tumor. In the days before surgery, Etta fasted and prayed. She was frequently tempted to believe the doctor rather than the assurance God had given her, but still, she remained steadfast.

How helpless and vulnerable Etta looked the day of her surgery, wrapped in a shapeless, colorless hospital gown! "I hope they know," I thought as I sat by her bed. "I hope these doctors and nurses know that they are dealing with the precious daughter of a powerful King!"

Of all the many Bible verses that Etta knows about healing and comfort, only one kept playing over and over in her spirit as she was wheeled into surgery: "Yea, though I walk through the valley of the shadow of death, I will fear no evil: for thou art with me" (Ps. 23:4, KJV). She was at peace.

Several hours later in recovery, Etta said she awoke to the nurse's voice saying, "Etta, wake up! You're okay! You still have your breast!" The doctor admitted later that he was truly surprised to find the tumor benign. Etta, however, was not.

If you asked her today to name her most precious experience with the Lord, Etta Edwards would not tell you a story of happiness or material blessing. She would tell again this story of testing and hope and the quiet confidence that brought her through a "fiery trial."

He Gives Us Comfort

Often during our hardships, the Lord will, for a time, wrap us in a warm and beautiful quilt of His consolation. "For in the day of trouble," says the psalmist, "He will conceal me in His tabernacle; In the secret place of His tent He will hide me; He will lift me up on a rock. And now . . . will I offer in His tent sacrifices with shouts of joy; I will sing, yes, I will sing praises to the Lord (Ps. 27:5–6).

Our friend Jandy Hanks says that she lives by the comfort of God these days. Jandy's wonderful husband, Bill, was struck down and killed by a hit-and-run driver over a year ago. Though Jandy had been a Christian for many years, through this tragedy she has found a new intimacy with the God she now knows as her "Abba"—her heavenly "Daddy." His comfort has not removed or even lessened her grief for Bill, but she says that it has been the quality of hope and life that has kept her alive. To all who know her, Jandy is an encouragement to trust in the promise of Jesus, "I will not leave you comfortless; I will come to you" (John 14:18, KJV).

I have never been more in touch with God's comfort in my own life than I was last August, sitting in the tiny intensive care unit where my sweet mother-in-law, Marjorie, lay dying. The compassionate team of nurses suspended hospital rules regarding the number of patients allowed to visit. For most of those last few days, all five of Marjorie's children and their husbands or wives were permitted to be with her. Though our hearts were breaking as we witnessed what we knew was the end of her life, there was tremendous joy at seeing one of God's own going forth to meet her precious Lord.

What a blessing we experienced as we stood together, softly singing to her the old hymns she so loved. At one point, a man in an adjoining I.C.U. room heard our singing and woke suddenly.

"Am I in heaven?" he asked his daughter as he struggled to sit up.

"Not yet, Papa!" she replied.

I still have a picture of the urgency in Marjorie's face as she regained consciousness for one brief moment. "We've got to tell them," she said to all of us gathered around her.

"Tell them what, Mama?" her daughter Debbie asked.

"We've got to tell them about His love," she said from a long way off, a vision of heaven in her eyes.

The love we felt for one another and for Marjorie during those last days together was intensified by the almost tangible presence of the Lord in that room. The comfort we received lifted us and gave us courage to face the period of grief that lay ahead.

He Gives Us Compassion

Through our times of tribulation, the Lord causes us to become tender and compassionate toward one another so that He may pour His healing through us to those around us. He allows us to share His suffering so that we may also share in the ministry of His healing:

For he gives us comfort in our trials so that we in turn may be able to give the same sort of strong sympathy to others in theirs. Indeed, experience shows that the more we share Christ's suffering, the more we are able to give his encouragement (2 Cor. 1:3–6, PHILLIPS).

J. R. Miller has said that unbroken men and women are of little use to God because they are deficient in their ability to love sacrificially. Miller contends that the whole business of this life is the learning of sacrificial, self-giving love. And this, he says, can best be learned through suffering.[10]

The trials we go through act as tutors in loving. They break into our stronghold of self-centeredness and open us up to the needs of others.

I was blessed to get to work with Joni Eareckson Tada on some lyrics for her first album, *Spirit Wings.* Joni, who became a quadraplegic in a diving accident at age seventeen, now works joyfully and tirelessly in a ministry to the handicapped. Her words and songs and paintings have influenced countless people for the Lord. She is nationally known and has traveled in many foreign countries as an advocate for handicapped people. Joni is quick to admit that God has taken her weakness and made it her strength. Through her surrendered suffering, He has poured out His compassion to millions in need.

On a smaller scale, I have seen the Lord work this redemptive principle in many lives around me. The area of suffering becomes the focus for a ministry of compassion. My mother, who suffered from depression, became motivated by her own problems to return to college at age sixty-two to study psychology. Mom is now a Ph.D. working with many women who suffer from problems that she once had.

Our friend Kym suffered abuse as a child and now works with other adults who were abused as children. Katherine (the mother of little Katie, who died after heart surgery) now works with Compassionate Friends, an organization for grieving parents. Valli and Brad, my sister- and- brother-in-law, who were unable to have children of their own, now have a houseful of adopted and foster children. My sister Alix, who has experienced the brokenness of divorce, now works as a counselor with those who have been similarly wounded.

A broken vessel is a powerful instrument in the hands of the Lord for this reason: It is through the "cracks" in our humanity that the healing oil of His indwelling Spirit is able to flow to His wounded world. Who better to speak words of hope and healing than one who has already walked the road of suffering?

Every one of us, to some extent, will experience suffering in this life. But praise God who is present in every circumstance— helping, healing, comforting, redeeming, drawing unexpected good from every evil. Praise our loving Father who is constantly urging us to move on past the painful question of "why?"— which looks backward—to the healing question of "what now, Lord?"—which reaches out in faith to all that lies ahead.

O FATHER GOD, we love You, and we trust You with our lives. We face whatever hard times may lie ahead confident in the fact that You have equipped us for the day of battle—and that You walk with us through every trial. We surrender to You the broken places in our lives. We surrender also the anger and confusion they have caused. Open our eyes, Father, to see that You are making us like Jesus. Open our eyes to see that You are shining through our brokenness, creating beautiful patterns of healing and wholeness. Open our hearts, Lord, to one another. Tune us in to the suffering that is all around us, that we may be the heart and the hands of your healing in this world. And give us, Father, a joyful expectancy for that great day when the suffering will be past and we will receive what you have promised us—a crown of life and "an eternal weight of glory" (2 Cor. 4:17). In Jesus' name we pray. AMEN.

Friend of a Wounded Heart

Smile—make 'em think you're happy,
Lie—say that things are fine,
And hide that empty longing that you feel—
Don't ever show it; just keep your heart concealed.

Why—are the days so lonely?
Where—can a heart go free?
And who will dry the tears that no one's seen?
There must be someone to share your silent dreams.

(Bridge)
Caught like a leaf in the wind, looking for a friend—
Where can you turn?
Whisper the words of a prayer, and you'll find Him there,
Arms open wide, love in His eyes!

(Chorus)
Jesus, He meets you where you are,
Jesus, He heals your secret scars,
All the love you're longing for
Is Jesus, the friend of a wounded heart.

Joy—comes like the morning,
Hope—deepens as you grow,
And peace beyond the reaches of your soul
Comes flowing through you, for love has made you whole.

(Bridge)
Once like a leaf in the wind, looking for a friend—
Where could you turn?
You spoke the words of a prayer, and you found Him there,
Arms open wide, love in His eyes!

(Repeat Chorus)

*Like the bits of glass in the kaleidoscope,
our lives are <u>colorful</u>.*

Confetti on Canvas 5
All the Colors of His Love

WHEN SPIKE AND I were struggling married students, supporting ourselves with part-time jobs, we did something wildly impulsive between semesters that we have never regretted. We took our tiny "nest egg"—such as it was—and flew to New York City just for the fun of it. What an incredible time we had! By taking advantage of bargain travel fares (middle of the night, middle of the week) and off-season hotel rates (would you believe $6.50 per night, one block from Times Square!), we were able to spend eight glorious days sightseeing, browsing old book shops and museums, and even taking in a few plays.

My memory of our first day in the Metropolitan Museum of Art is a little like an Impressionist painting itself—a beautiful blur of color and excitement. Like children at Christmas, we rushed eagerly into room after room of treasures, spending time in each to "unwrap" our discoveries.

About mid-morning, beginning to feel almost giddy from all the beauty we were taking in, we stumbled into yet another room of wonders, and there it was—Seurat's "Final Study of the Grande Jatte" (his last study in oil of the famous "Sunday Afternoon on the Island of the Grande Jatte").

The words in our mouths just kind of dried up, as we beheld the scene we had seen reproduced so many times in art books—the couple having a picnic, the lady with parasol and bustle, the little dogs, the children, and all that shimmering sunshine. A still and breathless hush seemed to fall over everything as we stood there, face to face with greatness.

There is no way to estimate how long we stood like that, not moving or talking. It was probably a matter of minutes, but it seemed much longer. Finally, timidly, we moved closer. I remember thinking, "this is the actual canvas that Georges Seurat put his actual brush to. The actual canvas!"

And that's when I noticed the "confetti"—the millions of tiny colored paint dots that the artist had placed carefully side by side to create this beautiful study in oil. The whole painting was made up entirely of little multicolored dots.

I had learned about this Neo-Impressionist technique in my art history class—"Pointillism," it was called. But seeing it in person was fascinating. Standing at close range, I found it difficult to discern the form and content of the painting. It seemed to be nothing more than an ocean of swimming dots—confetti on canvas. But when I pulled back, the familiar scene came into focus once more.

Since that day, I've sometimes envisioned God the Father as an artist and all of creation as His canvas. I can see each of our lives as a tiny dot of color in this great masterpiece He is creating. But He is the only One who has the "pulled back" perspective to see exactly what the painting will be. We're so involved and entangled in the world around us that we can't seem to get the "big picture."

But here's something interesting about the Father's giant "painting": Every dot within the picture is a tiny picture in itself—a masterpiece in its own right. And God alone knows what He is about as He adds the color and composition to each of our lives.

THE COLORS OF CREATION

Like the bits of glass in the kaleidoscope, like "confetti on canvas," our lives are indeed colorful. I think of this "color" as the beauty and creativity which God so generously puts into every life. Sometimes in the rush and confusion of my "dailiness," I fail to notice the color all around me. Or sometimes, when I am forced to struggle through a time of pain or grief, I become numb to it. But when I stop and purposely spend time getting in touch with the "color" God has put in my life, I find that two things happen: I please the heart of my Father, and I enrich the quality of my own life.

One fall morning not long ago, I really experienced the colors of God's love. It was one of those incredible mornings in

Alabama when the heart rejoices at the knowledge that summer really is *not* going to last forever—just when you thought it might! The first snap of a chill was in the air. I settled down in the den with my Bible and a cup of hot spiced tea to have a prayer time with the Lord.

Sometimes my time with the Lord can be quite a wordy affair, with my telling Him all sorts of things He already knows and stringing out long lists of requests for myself and others. But that morning (praise God!) my heart was full, and I was very still inside. For a long time I just sat there quietly, feeling His nearness to me and watching the beautiful array of birds flocking to our deck for the seed that Spike had sprinkled there.

Half a dozen bright blue jays competed noisily for their breakfast at the feeder, while about as many cardinals flapped in and out getting away with whatever they could steal from the competition. Two fat, gray, velvety doves waddled peacefully along the floor of the deck, pecking at the seeds which had spilled from the feeder overhead, and a red-breasted woodpecker propelled his technicolor body up and down the trunk of our Chinese Elm, pecking at its bark for bugs. A profusion of flowers (impatiens and salvia mostly) spilled from their pots in a riot of pinks and reds and purples. And all this against a sky so blue it might have been created from a first grader's crayon box.

I wrote in my journal that morning words that seemed to be an appropriate response to the beauty I beheld, although later, when I reread them, I saw them as a vast understatement. "Oh God," I wrote from my heart, "You did such a good job on your creation! Oh God, You did so good!"

These were words you might say in response to your child's arithmetic grade, not to the God of the universe in response to His magnificent creation. Yet somehow I knew that my words of admiration and praise were pleasing to the heart of my Father that day. I could feel His pleasure over my pleasure.

I think I understood something about God's love that morning that I had never known before—something about His desire for a relationship with us. When I create something that I think is good (whether it is a song or a meatloaf), I long to share it with someone. And I think God is like that. He has made this whole incredible world full of beauty and color and possibility, and He longs for us to look at it with wonder and appreciation. He longs to pour out on us all the wonder of who He is—to share His life with us in a love relationship. It must break His heart when we get so involved in the petty concerns of our own selfishness that we stumble blindly through this beautiful creation of His, never even noticing what He's put here for us.

In his beautiful creation psalm (Ps. 104), David pictures the Lord going about the work of making a world—"covering [Himself] with light as with a cloak, stretching out heaven like a tent curtain" (v. 2), making the clouds His chariot, and walking on "the wings of the wind" (v. 3). He describes the way that mountains and oceans and animals and birds came into being at the spoken word of our God. And in verse 24 he marvels at it all:

> O Lord, how many are Thy works!
> In wisdom Thou has made them all;
> The earth is full of Thy possessions,
> There is the sea, great and broad,
> In which are swarms without number,
> Animals both small and great. . . .
> They all wait for Thee.

What is David's response to all of this color and beauty? He decides in verse 33, "I will sing praise to my God while I have my being." Perhaps this spiritual response of David's is one of the reasons he is referred to in Scripture as "a man after [God's] own heart" (1 Sam. 13:14, Acts 13:22).

EARTH'S CRAMMED WITH HEAVEN

I know no one more tuned in to the beauty and color of God's creation than my husband, Spike. He delights in every change of season, in every bird and flower and bug—literally. (He's the only person I've ever known who tends and feeds garden spiders like pets!) One of the loveliest gifts he has given me in twenty-five years of marriage has been to open my eyes to the world around me. Having been gradually sensitized to the color and wonder of it all, I now find myself constantly amazed at how few people really notice the panorama of sights and sounds that God has set before us.

One of our favorite things to do on an autumn afternoon is to take a quilt down to the lake in the park behind our house and settle down to await the sunset flights of herons. There's a tiny island in the middle of the lake which has become the evening destination for hundreds of these varied and magnificent birds.

One night this fall, we sat silently together watching flight after flight of American egrets, snowy egrets, cattle egrets, little blue herons, and an occasional ibis coming in against an orange and purple sky. They would circle, dive, and flap into their selected places on the branches of a cypress near the island's edge, arranging their plumed bodies like so many live Christmas ornaments on an oversized tree. I somehow felt as though we were eavesdropping on a secret ceremony not meant for human eyes.

On the bank below us there was a lone fisherman, casting again and again into the black waters of the lake. "Look at him," Spike whispered. "He has never looked up once! There are angels dropping out of the sky, and he doesn't even know it!"

Elizabeth Barrett Browning once wrote,

> Earth's crammed with heaven,
> And every common bush afire with God.

I believe it is one of the great challenges of our humanity not to miss the heaven so close at hand. If we are ever to appreciate fully the outpouring of our Father's love, we must learn to look up from our ritual preoccupations and delight in the beauty He has set before us.

HUMAN SNOWFLAKES

I see the "color" of God's creation not only in the visual beauty of the world around me. I am also learning to see it in the incredibly diverse beauty of His children as well. Each of us has been made so uniquely, designed so specifically, that there is not one other person on earth exactly like us. We truly are what my friend Mickey Smith calls "human snowflakes." Every finger on every hand on every person in every land who has ever lived contains a unique fingerprint!

What a colorful creation this is! Think of it. God has delighted to give each one of us a special identity, and yet many of us spend our lives trying to conform to some self-imposed "norm." We deny our own individuality and that of others. We insist on playing out God's drama in black and white, ignoring the many colorful brushstrokes of His hand.

If there is any place on earth where creativity and individuality should flourish, it should be in the church of Jesus Christ. As the Holy Spirit is given full rein, each member of Christ's body should be moving toward the total fulfillment of his or her unique destiny. The separate gifts and abilities of each Christian should be lovingly sought out, coaxed, challenged, and encouraged by other members of the body.

Why is it then that I see so many "cookie-cutter Christians"? Why do whole churches full of God's people strive so hard to look and act exactly alike? I believe that in our efforts not to conform to the world, we in the church have made an unfortunate practice of conforming *to each other.* What a slap in the face to our Father who took such infinite care in making each of us a totally unique creation!

I thank God for the wonderful assortment of Christians who have influenced my life. Each one has added a layer of truth or insight or joy or understanding to my spiritual life.

John, our pastor, has what I call "the gift of the light touch" in his teaching. He can take what once seemed to be a stiff theological idea and move it, like a comfortable easy chair, into the living room of my heart, where I am able to live with it and use it every day.

Marshall, John's assistant, is gifted with such an orderly mind that he assimilates Scripture with the work of modern Christian writers into sermons that are both logical and passionate.

Pam, who teaches my Bible study, has a gift of discernment, which leads her, in counseling, to ask exactly the right questions— questions that have opened doors of spiritual growth for me.

And there are so many more . . . Laura makes me laugh and unlocks the joy that sometimes gets imprisoned in my serious side. Stephanie challenges me. Carolyn affirms and encourages me. Jacque listens with love. Martha, Sara, Becky, Kitty, Brennen, Nancy, Virginia, Jan . . . so many others.

Each has shaped my life in some positive way. Each has brought to me a part of God's love that no one else could have brought.

Suppose Mark, Luke, and John had all decided to write their Gospels from Matthew's perspective! Suppose James and Peter had decided to compose Epistles exactly like Paul's! God had something to say through each one of these lives that he could say through no other. And this is true of our own lives today. As the light of God's love shines through the "colored glass" of our own lives, He is forming patterns totally unique in composition and design.

ONE OF A KIND

As any parent knows, even children in the same family are unique individuals. And yet we are warned (unjustly, I feel) never to compare them. How can we possibly comply with that warning? Comparison is the most natural thing in the world. We compare everything else in our lives from the taste of foods to the prices of automobiles. What mother has not held her second newborn and thought, *He's lighter than the first* —or more serene, or darker, or more alert?

I feel that we parents should instead be encouraged to compare freely, but also to delight in the differences, whatever they are. We should learn to see each child not as a score on some plus-and-minus scale, but as a perfect creation of God's love.

Our two sons Curt and Andy are very different and always have been. Andy, the younger (now seventeen), is an extrovert who loves to be "where the action is" at all times. If he is not with one of his friends, he is on the phone with one. Hard-headed but tender-hearted, he has always been one to champion the "underdog," and he has a real love for pets and babies. Andy's talents lie in music, art, and writing. One of his most valuable assets is his sense of humor—he has been the family "comedian" since he could talk.

From Andy's scrapbook of writings, I love these "definitions" written for a fifth-grade assignment (I've left the spellings "pure"):

Friends: Friends are people who help you through hard times. Friends are people who will play with you when no one else will. Friends are people who's faces you always notice in the crowd because they're your friends.

School: Going to school is an experience in itself—not to be confused with really getting a normal education. (I don't think I'll read this out loud. I don't need that kind of trouble.)

Clothes: Pants are very nice
Pants are made with care
Pants require a fairly big price,
But without them you'd be bare.

Shirts can be admired
For everyone to see
But shirts are not required
In a nudist colony.

Underware is worn
By everyone I know
Who cares if it's torn
For it doesn't even show.

When you keep your clothes on
Some people think you're cute
But your best outfit grows on
It's called your birthday suit.

What do my parents think of me? My parents think that I am superbly wonderful, one of the most interesting people to be with, funny, that I have a good personality, I am super, not to mention great. All in all my parents think I'm one of the best kids that there is. (Parents don't know everything.)

Our older son, Curt, has a totally different personality. He has been a "deep thinker" since early childhood. In fact, I think he was a worried baby!

I remember seeing a Woody Allen film in which a young child is taken to a psychiatrist because he's not doing his homework. When questioned about it, the child answers, "The universe is expanding. What's the use?" Curt was a little bit like that at times. He had a way of contemplating things that I couldn't even understand, much less relate to—still does.

Of course, Curt has a definite fun-loving side, too. He's always up for a new experience or adventure, and he knows how to laugh at himself. But he feels things deeply, and he cares about the feelings of others. He's not much concerned with what the group thinks, and he tends to have his own opinions about everything.

Like his younger brother, Curt is talented in music, art, and writing, but because of his personality, his expression of these gifts is quite different. Here are some lines from a poem entitled "The Square Root of Nothing," which Curt wrote about God

when he was seventeen (he's eighteen now). In this poem he tells
all the things that God is to him and then admits that what he
"know[s] and can tell of God is still only the square root of
nothing":

> My God is an oak tree in the desert,
>   alone for 12,000 miles around;
>   with roots so deep and strong
>   they hold the earth in orbit;
>   and a trunk so sure and constant
>   to hold up the sky,
>   that it makes Atlas look like
>   Pee Wee Herman in Ethiopia.
> (Still, one time I carved "Curt loves God"
>   with my finger into His trunk,
>   and the sky moved)
> His branches are too wide
>   for infinity to imagine,
>   and I've climbed all over every one.

Two sons—with similar gifts but very different personalities.
What a mistake it would be to try to make the younger brother
into the older or the other way around (or worse yet, to try to
make them both into little clones of us)! And what a unique
treasure God has given us in each of them!

This is true of every person we know or see or encounter. Each
one of us is a one-of-a-kind masterpiece designed by God the
Father.

In 1982, I wrote with Ron Harris a musical entitled *One of a
Kind*, which was brilliantly performed in concert by Broadway
star Carol Lawrence. In it, the main character, Truly O. Jones (the
O stands for "Ordinary") is searching for her place in life—
searching for the thing that makes her special. One night just at
dusk she happens on to a traveling circus troupe which represents
the Body of Christ—a group called "E. Manuel's Masterpiece."
Each member of the troupe tries to help Truly discover her special
gift. The clowns hope that she'll have a gift for comedy. The
tightrope walker tries to develop her balance. The animal tamer
tests her courage.

Finally Truly makes friends with a very unusual character, a
two-headed man who is billed as "Jay-Ray, the double-dose of
entertainment." He helps Truly see that she'll never be happy

trying to be like other people. Her happiness will come when she
discovers that she, like Jay-Ray, is an original, "a masterpiece
made by the Master's hand."

In the end, all of the characters join in affirming the gift that
they have seen in Truly—the gift of encouragement. The characters then ask her to join the circus, and they give her a brand-
new name, "Truly Original Jones"! The musical closes with the
chorus of the title song "One of a Kind":

> One of a kind, Truly one of a kind—
> There's only been just one of you that's ever been designed!
> There's none other like you, or so I've been told,
> When God beheld what He had done, He broke the mold.
> One of a kind, Truly one of a kind—
> And you are just precisely what the Lord had in mind!
> Take a look deep down inside you, here is what you'll find
> Truly, you're one of a kind.[1]

There is tremendous freedom in our coming to the same realization that Truly came to. Accepting the fact that we are created
uniquely according to God's own blueprint can set us free from
self-criticism and self-hatred. And once we are free from self-
criticism, we can also be set free from judging others.

CELEBRATING GOD'S DESIGN

Last spring I attended one of Bill Gothard's seminars, which I
found very challenging. One of the parts of the seminar which
I appreciated most dealt with self-acceptance. Mr. Gothard encouraged each participant to inwardly accept the fact that "God is
building a unique life message in each of us," so that Christ may
manifest His life through our own uniqueness. We were asked to
think about the family traits, physical characteristics, or personality traits that we have felt ashamed of or wished that we could
change. (Freckles? Big feet? Fiery temper? I thought immediately
of my "bird legs" and my big ears!) Then we were encouraged to
spend time in prayer confessing our resistance to God's design for
our lives, asking Him to change what He felt needed changing and
accepting the rest as part of His perfect plan for us.

"Thou didst form my inward parts," says the psalmist. "Thou

didst weave me in my mother's womb. I will give thanks to Thee, for I am fearfully and wonderfully made" (Ps. 139:13–14). I am making this the prayer of my own heart as I learn to be more and more accepting of my uniqueness.

God is proud of His workmanship—delighted with each and every one of us, for each of us is truly a "masterpiece" to Him. Several Sundays ago I heard a sermon illustration, a wonderful parable that really brought this truth home to me.

It seems a famous artist was walking along the crowded streets of a large city far from his hometown. As he passed the open door of an art shop, he gazed in and there to his surprise saw a painting he had created years earlier. It was propped against the wall with several other old, dust-covered canvases. The color and detail he had once taken such pride in were now covered with years of age and grime.

The artist walked into the studio and, without even asking the price, offered the art dealer a large sum of money to buy back his own work. Carefully carrying the damaged treasure under his arm, he hurried back to his hotel, planning in his mind all the way how he would restore it to its original beauty.

You can guess the analogy, can't you? I am that damaged treasure, and so are you. Once created in all the brilliant colors of God's love, we have been soiled by our own sin and selfishness. We have been made drab by our resistance to God's unique and colorful plan for our lives. But our Father has paid the utmost price to buy us back and redeem us to His heart of love. We are that precious to Him.

O FATHER, thank You for all the colors of Your creation. And thank You that You have filled the world with the brilliant beauty of Your love. Open our eyes to see the diversity in Your creation not only in our surroundings, but in each other. Help us to appreciate and celebrate our own uniqueness and the uniqueness of our neighbor. Thank You, Lord, for buying back Your masterpiece with the price of Your only Son, our Savior, Jesus Christ. In Him we pray. AMEN.

Portrait of Jesus

Father, You are the artist with canvas and paint;
Color my life with Your blue skies and rain.
Paint seasons of sunshine and places of pain
'Til I am a picture of Him.

(Chorus)
Make me a portrait of Jesus,
Paint His love over my sin,
Let His life shine like a light through mine,
Make me a picture of Him.

Father, I am a canvas for You to create;
Capture the look of Your Son in my face.
But when You paint problems, Lord, frame them with grace
'Til I am a picture of Him.

(Repeat Chorus)

Father, You paint my future according to plan.
I trust You, though sometimes I don't understand
The rainbow of reasons that flow from Your hand
To make me a picture of Him.

(Repeat Chorus)

*Like the bits of glass in the kaleidoscope,
our lives are <u>transparent</u>.*

Windows in the Wall 6
Letting the Son Shine Through

THE MALL WAS TEEMING with shoppers. Every aisle and artery was clogged with panicked faces. Snowmen, Santas, shepherds, reindeer, wreaths, and ribbons of red and green inhabited windows and decorated doors. Carols clamored and competed with one another—"Mama kissing Santa Claus . . . in a one-horse open sleigh."

I was supposed to meet Spike at four, and here I was an hour early. So I settled down on a wooden bench outside Aladdin's Castle, where the bionic beeps and blips of video games punctuated the rest of the holiday chaos. "So this," I thought to myself, "is the season of joy."

Determined not to waste the hour, I took a notepad from my purse. I could at least get some writing done on my chapter, I thought . . . foolishly. In and out of my consciousness darted miniskirted teens giggling, weary toddlers whining, package-laden ladies bustling . . . and a partridge in a pear tree. I wrote, and scratched out, wrote, and scratched out, wrote, scratched out. It was useless. I couldn't make two words hold together. The confusion was siphoning off bits of ideas and pulling phrases apart. Why fight it? I returned notepad to purse, deciding to give in to the chaos around me.

A WALL OF CONFUSION

In some sense the above scene is a picture of everyday modern life. We are surrounded on all sides by competing sights, sounds, and stimuli of every variety. Canned music is piped into every

99

store and restaurant we enter, and it is impossible even to take an elevator ride in silence. Kids carry jam boxes along with them so they won't have to spend a single quiet moment alone with their own thoughts. And now with music videos, we need no longer rely on our imaginations for the visual content of songs—whole plots and dramas are provided for us.

All around us are the daily sounds of newscasters telling it like it is, traffic noises protesting the way it is, and politicians promising how it's gonna be. Every day we are finding it harder and harder to appropriate for ourselves even a shred of personal stillness. If what Elijah discovered is so, that the Lord speaks to us in a still, small voice, then it is no wonder so few of us are hearing Him!

If you were Satan and it was your job to distract the minds of men and women from the truth of God, what better scenario could you construct than the one we see all around us? It is as though the enemy has built a wall of noise and confusion between us and the quiet we require to hear our Savior speaking. Functioning like a spiritual Iron Curtain, this wall effectively separates many from God's good news on "the other side."

My friend Barb Voorhees, a missionary for Youth with a Mission, experienced the deadening reality of confusion-pollution working part of one summer in Manila, the teeming capital city of the Philippines. She and her co-workers were housed several to a room in a large, thin-walled building with only a faucet for a shower. But as primitive as the living conditions were, they were not the biggest hardship for Barb. Instead, it was the constant drone of city noises that bothered her most. Even when she was able to find time away from other people, she never felt totally alone with her own thoughts. The grinding of gears, the roaring of engines, the angry protests of automobile horns in the street outside filled her mind with a confusing undercurrent of sound that drained her spirit. Through this experience, Barb learned to treasure silence—real silence.

Most of us Americans don't live with the kind of cacophony Barb experienced in Manila. Still, we wake up, work, play, and go to bed to a background of low-level confusion—a confusion which competes constantly with the still, small voice of God and walls us off from Him.

What then is the answer? Transparency.

A TRANSPARENT LIFESTYLE

The Lord shines on this world He loves through the "transparent" lives of His children. He is waiting to make the life of each believer into a window in Satan's wall of confusion. If we are willing to stay transparent before Him, He can shine all the beauty and power of His own life through our lives (our circumstances and personalities). He can shine through us to all those who are trapped in darkness and chaos behind Satan's wall.

What does it mean to live a life that is transparent before God and man? Why should we desire it, and how do we achieve it?

I love the opening words of the Communion liturgy from *The Book of Common Prayer*: "Almighty God, unto You all hearts are open, all desires known, and from You no secrets are hid." Living transparently before God begins by acknowledging this—admitting that God is able to see through us anyway, whether we desire it or not. ("I, the Lord, search the heart, I test the mind. . . ." Jer. 17:10). We may clutter our inner lives with as many lies or exaggerations or self-justifications as we choose, but none of these is able to deter the eye of God from seeing right through to the heart of things in every life.

Living transparently means choosing to cooperate with this reality. It also means accepting a deeper truth—that the God who sees right through us loves us anyway. This, in essence, is the truth that sets us free!

I realize that I am a far cry from living transparently before God and man, but I fervently desire this quality in my life. I know only a few people who seem to possess it all the time, and I see in each of them a level of joy and serenity that I admire and long for.

If I were pressed to analyze a transparent lifestyle, I would say these things about it: (1) A person who lives transparently is committed to spending regular periods of *quiet* before God. (2) A person who lives transparently takes *confession* seriously. (3) A person who lives transparently has a *consistent* quality of Christlike behavior regardless of who or what she is dealing with.

QUIET: THE HIDDEN ROOM OF THE HEART

If we are to become windows in Satan's wall of confusion, we must be willing to pull away from that confusion for periods of *quiet reflection.* Lest we be conformed to the chaos around us, we must learn to seek in silence what Paul calls "the renewing of [the] mind" (Rom. 12:2).

Quiet time may be hard to come by in our busy lives, but finding it is worth our best efforts. Being silent in God's presence results in a clarity of vision and purpose that truly sets us apart from the strident clamor of this world.

Gordon MacDonald, in his book *Ordering Your Private World,* discusses what he calls "the sinkhole syndrome." Our lives under stress, says MacDonald, can become like the massive Florida sinkholes which caved in due to a drying out of underground springs. When we ignore the "underground," hidden world of prayer, our inner lives are subject to drying out and caving in.[1]

Even Jesus, the Son of God, needed regular times of silence in God's presence. He came to do only what His Father revealed to Him in secret (John 5:19–20, 30). And so hearing that still, small voice was vital to His life and ministry. Luke's Gospel tells us that "He Himself would often slip away to the wilderness and pray" (Luke 5:16).

If Jesus needed quiet times of communion with the Father, how much more do we. Only by pulling away into our hidden hearts to listen for the voice of our God can we experience Him deeply. There is a special room prepared within the heart of each believer which can only be unlocked by the key of silence. When we are willing to sit still, expectantly waiting, He will meet us there.

My experience of God's presence in times of silence are among the richest treasures of my prayer life. Why then am I so reluctant to be still?

I believe that everything in my flesh (that is, my natural, carnal self) pulls against my desire to operate in the Spirit. Jesus understood this very human tendency. When He encouraged the disciples to wait and watch with Him in the Garden of Gethsemane, He cautioned them that "the spirit is willing, but the flesh is weak" (Matt. 26:41).

Almost any time we decide to enter that secret room to be alone with God, we can expect to have something of an internal fight on our hands. It is as though the natural self is fighting for its life, knowing that to sit still in the presence of God is to be exposed to His penetrating light. M. Basil Pennington, in his book *A Place Apart,* contends that we avoid silence because "we do not want to be confronted with our hypocrisy, our phoniness.

We see how false and fragile is the self we project. . . . [Silence] is a harrowing experience, a journey, a death to self . . . and no one wants to die."[2]

My mind will invent a hundred pressing reasons to flee that silent room. Only when I ask the Spirit of God to fight my battle am I able to win out over the nagging urgency to run another load of wash or call a friend before she leaves for work. But once the struggle is finally over, I settle down into this gentle place of grace. Then I can feel an internal ebbing of confusion. Then and only then am I free to listen.

What happens in this silent room of my heart? Sometimes I will read from the Bible for a few minutes until I come across a passage that intrigues me. Then I ask the Lord to unlock this Word of His to me, and I wait expectantly.

Sometimes I will ask the Lord a special question, such as why I can't seem to love a certain person or how I can be a better parent to one of my children. During these times, I try not to deliberately "think." Instead I wait and listen. I picture myself seated in the presence of my Father, with His warm and healing light flooding over me.

Sometimes I begin with praise. I will sing a hymn or read a psalm, and then let my adoration fill the silent time. And there are other times when I enter the silence needing love and nothing more. I ask nothing. I tell nothing. I only climb up in my Father's lap and let Him hold me.

There is no foolproof formula. I have learned not to try to duplicate that "peak moment" I had last week. (Some ventures into silence will feel earthshaking and miraculous. Others will seem quite ordinary.) I try to come seeking the Lord and not the experience, and He always lets Himself be found. ("You will seek Me and find Me, when you search for Me with all your heart," Jer. 29:13.)

Though a time of silence with the Lord may lead into deep revelations about Scripture, it is not meant to replace Bible study. Though it may suggest needs for intercession or areas that need to be confessed, it is not meant to replace prayer. Though it may unleash within the heart awesome moments of adoration, it is not meant to replace praise. A time of silence is a separate discipline which reaps separate benefits.

Some days I integrate silence into my prayer and study time first thing in the morning. Other days I use silence separately as a little afternoon retreat in the midst of a chaotic day. But however I observe this time of silence, I invariably come away from it refreshed and renewed. I may have had the experience of receiving a specific answer to a specific problem; I may have received the comfort and strength of merely being in the Lord's presence. Even during spiritual "dry spells" when I didn't "feel" anything taking place, I still come away from my secret room more rested and content.

In the silence, the persistent clamor of "self" is tamed and quieted. The Spirit life grows strong and steady. As Scripture tells us, "in returning and rest shall ye be saved; in quietness and in confidence shall be your strength" (Isa. 30:15). Restful times of reflection in His presence build us up. They also draw back the curtains from our lives (God's "windows"), allowing Him to shine through.

CONFESSION: GOD'S PRICELESS GIFT

Perhaps God's most beautiful gift to the believer is His provision for forgiveness and reconciliation. It cost Him everything—the life and death of His Son. It costs us so little by comparison—only that we be willing to confess each wrong thought or deed or attitude and turn back to Him. Yet so often we let sins fester unconfessed beneath the surface of our lives.

One vital ingredient in our relationship with Jesus is our willingness to be honest with Him. He found it easy to be friends with harlots and tax collectors because they were honest with Him about their sinfulness. And He asks the same honesty of us.

Dietrich Bonhoeffer, in his book *Life Together*, suggests that grace and forgiveness are very difficult for the pious to understand. Only those of us who are willing to see ourselves as sinners will "catch on":

[Grace] says, You are a sinner, a great desperate sinner; now come, as the sinner that you are to God who loves you. He wants you as you are; He does not want anything from you, a sacrifice, a work; He wants you alone. "My son, give me thine heart" (Prov. 23:26). God has come to you to save the sinner. Be glad! The message is liberation through truth. You can hide nothing from God. The mask you wear before men will do you no good before Him. He wants to see you as you are, He wants to be gracious to you. You do not have to go on lying to yourself and your brothers, as if you were without sin; you can dare to be a sinner. He loves the sinner, but He hates sin.[3]

Christians whose lives are transparent before the Father see themselves as sinners. They understand grace and praise God for it. Because they know that their forgiveness was not bought cheaply, they take it very seriously.

Transparent Christians keep "short accounts" with God and other human beings, confessing their sins frequently and obtaining forgiveness. It is this process of honestly confessing before God and receiving His forgiveness that keeps us (His "windows") washed so that the light of Christ may shine through.

I had not been a committed Christian very long before the Lord let me learn firsthand about the power available to me through complete honesty with Him. I had agreed to have Andy's little friend Ernie stay with us over a Saturday night while his parents went out of town for a football game. It was really not a convenient time for me, since we were entertaining that Saturday. But his mother had sounded desperate, so I had said yes and hoped for the best.

I planned to do most of my dinner party preparations on Friday afternoon and night so I could devote Saturday to Andy and his guest. Imagine my surprise when Ernie's mom arrived at my door with child and suitcase in tow a whole day early. She said she was sure I had understood that Ernie was to be with us all weekend instead of just one night!

I was so stunned that I could hardly respond as she and her husband drove off waving cheerily. It was not too many minutes before my shock began to turn to anger. I felt used and taken advantage of. (Poor little Ernie. I'm sure he didn't understand why there was smoke coming out of my ears!)

By God's grace I recognized this anger as sin right away, but I seemed powerless to do anything about it. I felt so justified, so righteously indignant, that the anger would flare back up as soon as I confessed it. I couldn't stomp it out or smother it, though I tried.

I left Ernie settled in front of the television set waiting for Andy to return from school while I walked out into the backyard clenching my fists.

"Lord, this is ridiculous. It's not that big a deal. I shouldn't be this angry, but I'm out of control. What do I do?" I pleaded.

"Don't tell Me how you should or shouldn't be," He seemed to say. "Tell Me how you *are.*"

"How I am? I don't understand."

"Tell Me exactly what you're feeling right now," was His silent invitation.

"Well . . ." I began hesitantly, "I'm mad. I'm really mad! I'm furious!" I growled. Now I was getting worked up. "I feel used. It was not a good time for company anyway, and now she's dumped her kid on me for two nights instead of just the one she asked for. It's not fair." Just like a river of poison the words of resentment were pouring out. I was pacing up and down by now. "Lord, I know it's wrong to stay mad, but I don't know where to put my anger. I've confessed it, and I know You forgive it, but it won't go away. What am I supposed to do?"

"Could you love this child for Me?" asked the still, small voice. "Could you keep him and care for him . . . for Me?"

"For You?" I asked.

"Yes. If not for his mother, could you take him into your home without resentment and give him love because *I* have asked you?"

As simply as that my heart was turned around. I suddenly saw the truth that it was God who had brought Ernie to our house for the weekend. He had his reasons. Perhaps I was even entertaining an angel unaware (Heb. 13:2)! I knew then that I could love Ernie for his heavenly Parent even if I still felt anger toward his earthly one.

As I went back inside and got out the cookies and milk, I actually found myself praising God. My heart was filled with a peaceful awareness of His involvement in all of my plans, of His care for my smallest cares and His concern for my real feelings. Regardless of Ernie's mother's motives, my commitment to love and serve had been made to God, and I could honor it. Silently I bundled up my anger and placed it on His altar. And He took it.

How blessed we are to have a Father who knows us so well and loves us anyway! A Father who will not reject us for our real feelings, but will take the time to sort through them with us, helping us to change each sinful attitude. He's not interested in a superficial relationship based on "shoulds" and "oughts." He wants us to "get real" with Him so that He can be real to us.

Richard J. Foster, in his book *Celebration of Discipline,* states this so well: "The Discipline of confession brings an end to pretense. God is calling into being a church that can openly confess its frail humanity and know the forgiveness and empowering graces of Christ. Honesty leads to confession, and confession leads to change."[4]

CONSISTENCY: MERE SIMPLICITY

Consistently Christlike behavior is the distinguishing characteristic of transparent Christians. Their choices are dictated by an inner consciousness, rather than by any set of outer circumstances. Their manner and conversation are essentially the same regardless of who they're with at any given time.

Surely you can think of a few precious people like this in your life. I think of Katherine Deaton, whose manner is gracious and gentle whether she is dealing with the members of her Bible study group or the inmates in her prison ministry. I think of Roland Phillips, who treats my teenagers with as much respect as he does his employers at the law firm. I think of Jack Truitt, whose kindness and humor extend far beyond his personal friendships—to hotel bellmen and waitresses and anyone else fortunate enough to encounter this lovable bear of a man.

I love these words of Sören Kierkegaard, which picture a consistently transparent life: "If thou art absolutely obedient to God, then there is no ambiguity in thee and . . . thou art mere simplicity before God."[5]

To live consistently, transparently, is "mere simplicity" because when we live like that we allow Christ to do the work in our lives —the choosing, the acting, the loving. We see our lives as "windows" and merely allow His light to shine through our uniqueness. Our words and actions spring from His indwelling life. It is that simple.

But it doesn't always *feel* simple, especially if you are a "people pleaser," as I have been for much of my life. Growing up, I desired more than anything else the love and respect of other people, and I found out early on that I was a very good actress. So here was my *modus operandi:* If I wanted you to like me (which I did), I would try to find out what kind of person you liked, and then I would *act* like that.

For example, the summer I turned fifteen I went to church

camp for two weeks. As usual, from the moment I arrived my "antenna" was out to discover how I should act in order to get the most love and admiration from my fellow campers—a brand-new audience.

Sizing things up, I decided (on a fairly unconscious level, you understand) that "funny" was the thing to be—the person who could get the most laughs could have the most friends. So I developed this "act"—I would "play" this character who always made a dumb remark. And it must have worked—everyone seemed to think I was hilarious.

The boys especially seemed to like my "act." Sometimes one boy would bring several of his friends over to my table in the "chow hall" to display my dumbness. He would bait me with a trick question just to see what flaky answer I would come up with. Then they would all die laughing. I loved the attention, which I think I must have equated with admiration.

That summer when camp favorites were elected, a whole new category was created just so I could be elected; it was entitled "The Bum Dunniest." Since my nickname that summer was "Bum Dunny," I'm sure no one else got any votes in this special dumb category! "Wonderful," I thought when I was elected. "I'm a camp favorite!"

But then came the last evening worship service of the summer, held as usual in a beautiful open pavilion in the woods. That night the speaker was my favorite preacher on staff, a bright, intuitive man named John Jenkins, and his topic was humility.

At some point during the sermon that night, the electricity in the pavilion went out, and we were left sitting in total darkness with the sounds of the night all around us. The words of the sermon seemed to come out of nowhere and go straight into my heart. They spoke about the importance of understanding who we really are in Christ.

"Who we really are." That phrase soaked into me. Though I can't say that I understood the gospel that night, I did understand something else. With great sadness I realized that I had missed the opportunity to build any honest friendships that summer. I had been so busy constructing a persona my "friends" would find amusing that I had never even given them a chance to know me—the real me. And the scariest part of this whole insight was to realize I wasn't even sure that *I* knew "the real me."

The memory of that summer is an emotional one. I realize that in many ways I am still that insecure girl—still on a pilgrimage toward self discovery, as many of us are.

For Christians, the most important step on that journey is learning to accept the Lord's acceptance. His acceptance of us makes knowing ourselves safe and loving ourselves possible.

Once we see and accept who we are in His eyes, we can begin to share ourselves honestly, transparently, with others, allowing the Lord's light to shine through us. Then, too, can we begin to see Him shining through others.

Let me share with you a modern-day parable recorded in the beautiful prose of my husband's journal. Spike was raised in the church and had heard of Jesus all his life, but for years the Lord remained abstract to him, and somehow impersonal. Then gradually, beautifully, as Spike began to seek a deeper relationship with Jesus, the Lord began to reveal Himself in the faces and lives of other people. Through many different "windows" Spike has begun to see the face of Christ, and it is changing his life. Here he tells of one such instance:

Saturday, 3 May 1986. Here is a thing I saw at the state track meet that speaks of the fragrance of God. It could begin as a parable—as in "The Kingdom of God is like . . . two deaf runners in a two-mile race."

I was there to see Curt run, and I had positioned myself [near] one of the gates. . . . The stadium was filled with track teams from all over the state, each having selected its own place in the stands . . . the bright colors of their running clothing like a patchwork quilt spread out in the sun. . . . It was a beautiful spring day, cloudless and warm, with just a hint of a breeze. I was relaxing in the sun, with an hour's wait before Curt's next race, observant to the events going on all around me—immersed in the drama of man rather than in the drama of nature (my usual perspective). . . .

[Here Spike describes in detail a two-mile race in which a large number of runners (the best two from each district) competed. He explains that usually there are not large gaps between the finishers, since all are state-qualifying runners.]

. . . But for Alabama School for the Deaf, such was not the case. . . . [Their two runners] had finished dead last . . . almost a full lap behind the winner. I watched these two strong, handsome black teenagers cross the track after the race, slow of step, exhausted, eyes downcast in embarrassment. Climbing the steps to face their teammates, they were the essence of broken spirit.

Suddenly, bounding down the steps to meet them came their

coach, a plump little man a good two inches shorter than either boy. As the two runners approached him on the stairs, the first of the two raised his head and looked at his coach with such an expression of brokenness on his sweating face that I could scarcely bear it, and the second young man actually backed down a couple of steps and stood with head bowed, barefooted, shoes in hand, utterly low and dejected.

As he reached the first runner, the coach literally enfolded the boy with an enormous hug. Then, holding him at arms' length and looking him directly in the face, he spoke these words very distinctly and loudly: "YOU DID A FINE JOB FOR ME IN RUNNING THAT HARD RACE, AND I WANT TO THANK YOU FOR IT. I LOVE YOU, AND I AM VERY PROUD OF YOU!"

The runner looked unblinkingly at the coach's mouth, straining to read the words on his lips. As the meaning of those words gradually dawned on the boy, I watched a smile cover his whole face—a smile that was a joy to see.

The coach then bounded down the steps to where the second, even more dejected runner waited to face the criticism I'm sure he felt he deserved. Another hug and straightforward full-eye contact. Then the coach put his mouth close to the deaf boy's ear (his deafness was evidently not as complete as the first runner's). The words he spoke were loud enough that I and anyone else within fifteen yards could hear them clearly: "MARTIN, I AM VERY PROUD OF THE RACE YOU RAN. I TOLD YOU THAT WE COULD HAVE OUR BEST TIME EVER IN THIS MEET, AND WE DID. YOU RAN AS HARD AS YOU COULD. I LOVE YOU, AND I AM PROUD TO BE YOUR COACH."

The coach turned and accompanied the boy up the steps past where I was sitting, his arm around him, patting him all the way. As they came past me I could see that the boy was totally transformed, his exhausted body now straight, his head held high with renewed strength and confidence, his very spirit restored.

And so once again I saw Him. Jesus. Clothed in green and yellow polyester shorts and shirt, with a stopwatch around his neck, coaching Alabama deaf runners, right there in Troy, Alabama, in broad daylight for anyone to see.

"I love you and I am proud to be your coach" is what He said. The fragrance of the Lord, the sweet smell of that moment, comes back to me each time I remember it."

FATHER, help us to live more and more openly before You. This world so desperately needs to see You. Let it be through us. Be present to us as we seek You in the silence. Be merciful to us as we bare our hearts to You in confession. And as we behold "with open face" the glory of Your Son, change us more and more into His image, until our words and thoughts and actions are consistent with His. Father, thank You for making us windows in the wall of this world's confusion. Shine through us, Lord, bringing light into the darkness. We praise You and bless You. We ask all of these things in the precious name of Jesus. AMEN.

Windows

There's a wall that stands between the Lord
And people in the darkness;
It is built of Satan's lies, and it must fall.
But the love of God can find a way
To shine into the darkness
When we let our lives be windows in that wall.

(Chorus)
We are windows,
Windows for the world to see Jesus —
That's what He's calling us to.
We are windows,
Windows that His love has thrown open,
Windows for His life to shine through,
Windows for the world.

Somewhere there's a child in need
Who's crying in the darkness,
Somewhere there's a man who's in the dark,
Somewhere there's a woman
Who will never see the sunshine
Unless we take His light into their hearts.

(Repeat Chorus)

Like sunshine through the kaleidoscope, the light of Christ shines through our lives.

A Million Mornings 7
Light Is a Person

THE MINUTE I SAW THE ROOM, I knew I was going to love school. The kindergarten was huge and sunny and filled with wonderful things. There were two book tables piled high with colorful picture books and a block corner with stacks of smooth wooden blocks for building. Along the window wall, a tiny kitchen was equipped with furniture, appliances, pots, pans, and dishes just the right size for five-year-old "housewives." At the far end of the room were two large rectangular easels holding trays of tempera paints and soft, wide brushes. There was a toy bin, a record player, and a shelf full of rhythm instruments—cymbals, tom-toms, triangles, a xylophone, and several tambourines. Even my teacher was beautiful. Her name was Miss Johnston, and she had a smile for everyone.

I loved everything about kindergarten—even science. There were no textbooks with intimidating terms or theories, only feathers and birds' nests and colored leaves and wildflowers and a wonderful ant farm in an aquarium.

My favorite thing about science was the experiments. I remember one experiment in particular where we took two identical plants and set out to discover the effect of sunlight on growing things. We set one on a window sill where it was bathed in light all day. The other was placed in a cupboard in total darkness. At regular intervals we watered both plants. And we watched.

Of course you know the results—you went to kindergarten, too! The plant in the window flourished—grew taller and put out new, green leaves. Periodically we would gather around the cupboard at the back of the room and wait breathlessly to observe the fate of the poor plant in exile. It became pale and stunted and quite pathetic. My young heart went out to that plant in the cupboard. It hardly seemed fair (even for the sake of science) to warp its whole little life just to satisfy our curiosity.

CREATED FOR LIGHT

Like those plants in my kindergarten experiment, we too were created for Light. Our spirits crave and cry out for the nourishing Light of Christ. Without it, we become inside like the plant in the cupboard—pale and anemic and stunted. We may look fine on the surface; we may work and wear the right clothes and smile and seem pretty much okay. But deep down where the spirit part of us dwells, without Jesus we are dying.

When the musical *Everlasting Light* was in the planning stages, several of us who were to be involved with the project at Word committed to studying the "light verses" in the Bible as a foundation for our work. We found that "light," as it is spoken of in Scripture, is almost always a figurative word representing *the Son of God* ("I am the light of the world," John 8:12); *the Word of God* ("Thy word is . . . a light unto my path," Ps. 119:105); *the Law of God* ("the law is light," Prov. 6:23, KJV); or even *the people of God* ("You are the light of the world," Matt. 5:14). It is also used to point to *qualities or gifts of God,* such as wisdom (Eccl. 2:13); salvation (Ps. 27:1); healing and health (Isa. 58:8); glory (Luke 2:32); prophecy (2 Pet. 1:19); and eternal life (Isa. 60:19).

I recall those weeks of work on *Everlasting Light* as a real time of spiritual growth for me. But it was also a time of tremendous struggle. It seemed that every power of darkness was pulling against my efforts to glorify the Light. Everything went wrong. I lost things, like a whole huge section of the manuscript which had not yet been entered into the word processor. I had scheduling conflicts. I was even taken to the hospital in Waco, Texas, with a severe migraine headache the day of our most important planning session. I know it was the prayer support and encouragement of many believers (especially my friend Pam Norton and my sister-in-law, Tish) that kept me going.

During those weeks of darkness, I learned a lot about the Light. I was forced to walk by faith much of the time when things seemed pretty dark and progress was not easily made.

And I learned to stay focused on God's Word—especially on His glorious promises of Light.

THE ROAD OUT OF DARKNESS

In the kaleidoscope metaphor, as in the Bible, God is the Light. He is the One who brings meaningful patterns out of the brokenness and confusion of our lives.

John, in his beautiful first Epistle, says that "in Him there is *no* darkness at all." None. If we say we love God and yet continue to stumble around in the same dark corridors of our own sinfulness, we're just fooling around—fooling ourselves and others, or trying to. As John puts it, we're lying, for we don't know God at all.

But once we've given our lives to Him, once we've stepped over into His kingdom of Light, then (wonder of wonders) we have fellowship with God and with one another! We're bathed in His own holiness and cleansed with His perfection. We have something incredible that we could never obtain apart from that Light. We have righteousness—a right and perfect relationship with Him (1 John 1:5–10).

The roadmap of every Christian journey is alike in this way: It leads, by whatever winding path, from darkness into Light.

Your darkness and mine may take a different form. There is the devastating darkness of crime, the illusive darkness of compulsive behavior. There is the darkness I lived in—the subtle, devious darkness of self-centeredness that traps us in a maze of egocentric pursuits. There is the darkness of spiritual pride, a trap for many "good" Christians. In this shadow land of Phariseeism, doing the right things for the wrong reasons draws us deeper and deeper into the black swamp of hypocrisy.

The kind or degree of darkness is not the issue. *Anything* that separates us from the warming, healing sunshine of Jesus Christ is sin, for in Him there is no darkness at all.

I don't pretend to be a religious expert. I'm certainly not a theologian. But I have walked in darkness and then have turned around and walked in light—and I know the difference. I know the One who *is* Light, and He is the difference.

My lyric to "Light of a Million Mornings" says it this way:

I've never tried to understand a sunrise;
I only know it takes away the dark.
I can't explain Your healing, or all the joy I'm feeling;
I only know You've come into my heart.[1]

It doesn't take a degree in theology to be an expert on Light. As my old friend Josephine used to say, "Every Christian is an expert on this one thing—'what *my* God has done for *me.'* On this subject no authority in the world can question you." And in this Light, I *am* an expert, and so are you—if you know Him.

HOMESICK FOR THE SUNSHINE

The trouble is, so many don't know Him—and even those of us who do sometimes lose sight of Him. When God thought us up, when he put together His whole bright and beautiful world, He created us to walk in Light, to share with Him all the beauty and wonder of the green Garden. But we chose instead to investigate the darkness by following our own way. And since the time of that first rebellion, darkness has been thick over the world and its people.

Not too many years ago, Spike and I were in Manhattan again. This time the trip was partly business, partly pleasure. I had looked forward to getting away from the busy routine of household and children. I couldn't wait to spend time alone with Spike, seeing a few plays, doing some shopping, and ending the week with a jaunt into the surrounding countryside to enjoy the autumn leaves. Our plan had been to spend five days in the city and two in the country, but it didn't work out quite that way.

Somehow the "darkness" of the city seemed overwhelming to me that trip. It was more than the gray, rainy weather. Perhaps it was my imagination, but I seemed to sense a sadness in the eyes of the people all around me—the crumpled, ragged bag ladies, the pin-striped executives, the haggard-faced doorman at our hotel, the well-heeled hobnobbers at the Russian Tea Room. It kept occurring to me that this whole assortment of humanity, every man and woman of them, had been created to walk in the Garden with the Lord in the cool of the day, but many of them hadn't even heard that rumor. Instead, they were trapped here in the dark, rain-soaked city, destined to take subways and side streets and dead-end alleyways to nowhere. I persuaded Spike to get me out of the city and onto the country roads of Connecticut ahead of schedule. I felt like my heart was breaking. I needed some sunshine.

I'll never know how much of the sadness I saw that trip was real and how much was imagined. Certainly cities do not hold the copyright on darkness! But I have never forgotten that trip or my grief over what I saw as God's lost creation.

I was reminded of my experience in the dark city when I read Frederick Buechner's wonderful essay, "Adam," in his book, *Peculiar Treasures*. In the essay, Buechner poignantly describes a modern-day Adam, a city-dweller, who is homesick for the light of a Garden he has never even seen.[2] Buechner's essay moved me to write a lyric about this contemporary Adam living in darkness:

ADAM

He wonders why they call it news—
Same old story, same old gory details.
He puts the paper down and lights a cigarette.
T.V. blaring through the walls,
Rerun laughter in the after hours,
And that sad familiar memory that he can't forget.

The garden was green, the water was clean
The animals came without names,
And love was a girl who walked through a world
Where passion was pure as a flame.
In the dark of his mind is a time before time
And a sad irreversible fact . . .
He can't seem to think how he lost it,
And he can't seem to find his way back.

He drains his third martini glass,
Mem'ry stirring, finally blurring dimly.
He tells himself again that it was for the best.
He looks out on the rainy streets—
Lines of traffic seem a tragic image
And the sweet familiar scene inside his head won't rest.

The garden was green, the water was clean
The animals came without names,
And love was a girl who walked through a world
Where passion was pure as a flame

In the dark of his mind is a time before time
And a sad irreversible fact . . .
He can't seem to think how he lost it
And he can't seem to find his way back.[3]

In a very real sense, we are all Adams and Eves who have strayed from the Garden. Rather than remaining in the circle of God's perfect love, we have been lured out into the no man's land of our own self-centeredness. We have been drawn into the darkness rather than basking, like healthy plants, in His perfect Light.

But what exactly is "His perfect Light"? It is certain to remain a totally abstract concept until we see what power it can have for us personally. This transforming life-force of Jesus, this dynamic outpouring of His truth and love which is represented by the image of "light," must be experienced to be fully understood.

I'm sure I'm not even aware of all the various ways that His Light is operating in my life, but I *am* aware of a few that I can describe in specific, concrete terms.

LIGHT FOR THE STEP AHEAD

The Light of Christ acts in my life as a personal guide, a compass, a "tour director" if you will, giving me moment-by-moment wisdom about how to proceed on my journey. In Psalm 119, the Psalmist describes the Word of God as a "lamp unto my feet and a light unto my path" (v. 105). I get a picture of a night traveler stepping out into some wild, uncharted territory with only a lantern for light. I have found the Light of Christ to function a lot like that in my life—faithfully supplying me with just enough vision to take the next step.

Many times I would love to see the whole journey lit up before me on a huge video screen. I would love to be forewarned of every hazardous turn and every lurking danger. Instead He illumines only one step at a time. But the good news is: I don't have to take that step alone. He is walking right beside me all the way!

As God gave fresh manna to the Israelites one day at a time, He supplies His Light (wisdom, guidance) for the dark times of our lives in daily (sometimes hourly) doses—just enough light for each encounter or situation.

I have taken tremendous comfort, for example, in His promise to supply us with the right words to speak in each circumstance. We are not to ponder or fret or stew over what our response will be, but instead to trust Him to supply the answer we need when the question is asked (Luke 12:11–12).

Trusting God's Light to be sufficient for every dark place as we move forward is a good description of "walking in the Spirit." I am learning to give up my own rigid plans in favor of His sometimes spur-of-the-moment ones as I learn to follow His Spirit.

Recently I had a chance to exercise my trust in God's guiding light. It began as a challenge from the prayer-study-fellowship group that Spike and I lead in our home on Monday nights. This delightful assortment of "brothers and sisters" from our church is fast becoming a real family for us as we encourage each other to find ways of living out the gospel every day. The week after Christmas we had a wonderful evening together studying the second chapter of Philippians. A meaty discussion on what it means to be a servant led us to make this commitment to each other for the following week: We agreed to ask the Lord each morning whom we could serve for Him that day.

Tuesday morning bright and early, I settled down for my quiet time. I knew I had to ask the question; I had promised the others I would. But I had lots of writing to do that day, and I wasn't feeling much like a servant.

"Lord," I said hesitantly, "Is there anybody that you want me to serve today? Because if there isn't, that would be fine, too. I can check with you again tomorrow."

As I sat quietly, I began to think about my friend, Laura. Her baby was due in eight days, and there had been workmen at her house every day for weeks hammering, painting, and creating confusion as they completed the new den and office addition to her house.

"Call Laura," the Spirit seemed to be saying. "She could probably use some help."

Laura's voice on the phone was one part frantic, two parts tired. "We're trying to move all of the books out of John's old study to get it ready for the baby," she explained.

When I relayed this information to Spike, he agreed that this was undoubtedly our "call" to serve that day. We packed a lunch for four and arrived on John and Laura's doorstep within the hour for book-moving duty. What a fun, funny day we had with our friends turning an office into a nursery! By the time we left them late that afternoon, we had torn down and transported a desk and two file cabinets, relocated hundreds of books, and had about a million laughs!

We didn't know, when we went to sleep that night, exactly how perfect the Lord's timing had been. The phone rang just before dawn the next morning.

"We're at the hospital," John told us breathlessly. "Laura went into labor about midnight, and it shouldn't be too much longer!"

I'm so thankful we didn't ignore the "light" the Lord gave us about how to serve Him that day. Because we followed Him, Laura was able to go to the hospital confident that the nursery was cleared out and waiting for the new baby.

This was not a special or unusual case. There's no doubt in my mind that the Lord is trying to give us this kind of "light" in hundreds of situations every day, but we are either too busy to ask Him or too preoccupied to hear.

LIGHT AT THE END OF THE TUNNEL

Another way the Light of Christ works in my life is by bringing me hope. How in the world do people raise their children (especially their teenagers) without this priceless gift of grace?

My journal is full of what I call "SOS entries" that only the parent of a teenager can understand:

26 September 1987. Lord, I'm stumped—I really am. I feel like a bundle of frustrations with clothes on. I can't do it. I can't love well enough or hard enough or true enough to get through to him. I can't melt this wall he has constructed with his cold words and his rebellious looks. It's got to be Your love, Father. Mine hasn't got an ounce of power.

4 November 1987. Father, this is a major revelation! Why did it take me so long to see it? I can't do this motherhood gig in the flesh! It's *got* to be in the Spirit or it won't work!

18 January 1988. Andy's music is blaring overhead as he showers. The voice sings over and over, "And I still haven't found what I'm looking for." Night before last a boy from Murphy High School that he and Curt knew killed himself. . . . Did no one even know how badly this child was hurting? . . . Oh Lord, the power of this world is so ruthless. It looks to gobble up the defenseless ones. Protect my children. Draw them to You, Father.

On days like these (and there are lots of them), the darkness moves in so close that it's difficult to see even one step ahead. That is when Jesus gives me hope for what lies out beyond the darkness. He is the Light at the end of the tunnel. I know His word, I believe His promises for me and my family, and I can keep going even when the darkness seems to be closing in.

Recently when my friend Barbara and I were praying for my children, she showed me a wonderful way to appropriate God's Light for dark, difficult times.

"Ask the Lord to show you who Curt and Andy were designed to be in the Body of Christ," she said. "What are the gifts that God has given them for the good of the kingdom? Get hold of a vision of who they will be when God finally has His way, and then pray toward that goal."

This is a wonderful way to pray. The Lord will give us the faith to take in stride the problems and frustrations that surround us so that we can look ahead to the "finished product." His Light supplies the hope we need to see our prayers as already answered. And this "light-at-the-end-of-the-tunnel" prayer is not only for teenagers! It is helpful in any situation where the answer seems a long way off.

Some years ago, I was so encouraged by a brief article in a Christian magazine that I clipped it out for my permanent "motherhood file." It told the story of a mother who had prayed for her son from his infancy, believing that the Lord had a plan for his life. The boy grew up and went off to college. Once on his own, he made some sadly destructive choices for his life. He got involved in a strange Eastern religion; he moved in with a woman and had a son out of wedlock.

Though heartbroken, the mother clung to her belief in God's promises for her child and persisted in prayer. Years went by. Her son gave up the woman he had lived with, but he kept the child. Once on a visit to her son, the mother found him hungry to know about God. He even asked for her prayer, received the Lord, and was baptized.

Within a year, the mother died. According to the article, "she never got to see with earthly eyes the great man of God her son became," never heard his powerful sermons or read his great books. And then the surprising conclusion to this article revealed that the woman was Monica and her son was Augustine, the great fourth-century theologian and leader of the early church.[4]

This mother-and-son story had such a contemporary ring to it, it could have happened today in your hometown or mine. Reading it, I realized that people have not changed, sin has not changed, and the victorious power of God's love to heal and redeem has not changed. We, like the faithful Monica in the story, can keep our eyes on the light of God's promises as we pray and hope for our children.

If we could see the future lit up on a huge video screen, we wouldn't need hope, would we? ". . . For why does one also hope for what he sees? But if we hope for what we do not see, with perseverance we wait eagerly for it" (Rom. 8:24–25). We who know and believe the Lord have read the last chapter of the Book, and we are able to hang on to the promise of that glorious finale. We possess the faith of Hebrews 11 which is "the assurance of things hoped for, the conviction of things not seen" (Heb. 11:1).

The world around us is perishing for just a taste of the promise, just a glimmer of the hope in our hearts. And the good news is this: It's *very* contagious! God will give us the boldness to rise to Peter's challenge: "Always [be] ready . . . to give an account for the hope that is in you" (1 Pet. 3:15). And as we begin to share our hope, we can watch the Lord be born again and again and again into the hearts of those around us. The Light that sheds hope is a great blaze which is spread from one tiny candle to another:

> One candle lights one candle,
> Two candles light four,
> And where they shine
> There is no darkness anymore.
> Two candles light four candles,
> Four candles light eight,
> And in the light of Jesus
> We can celebrate![5]

LIGHT THAT LEADS TO HOLINESS

There is another surprising way I feel the light of Christ working in my life. It is drawing me (slowly but surely!) to holiness.

I must confess right up front that holiness was not something I thought I wanted or needed before I knew the Lord. To me, it was a prissy, stuffy, old-fashioned notion, totally inapplicable to anybody living in this century. If I had ever thought much about the word *holy* (which I didn't), I think I would have defined it as "unimaginative, impractical, and boringly goody-goody."

Even after becoming a committed Christian, I felt almost positive that even God could not desire or require anything as antiquated as holiness from the people He loved. ("Good," maybe, or "better," but certainly not "holy.") It only took a glance or two at His Word to convince me otherwise. Holiness, it seems, figures very strongly in God's plans for us, His people.

Paul says in his letter to the Ephesians that Jesus chose us before the foundation of the world to live as adopted children of the kingdom, "holy and blameless" (Eph. 1:4–5). He tells the Colossians that God the Father gave His best to reconcile us to Himself through the blood of His Son. And why? So that we could be "holy and blameless and beyond reproach" (Col. 1:9–22). Peter writes in his first Epistle, "But like the Holy One who called you, be holy yourself also in all your behavior" (1 Pet. 1:15).

You may be thinking what I'm thinking as I reread these verses: "It's a great plan, Lord, but how in the world do You ever expect us to pull it off? People just can't make themselves holy."

And it's true—no educational system, no scientific discovery or medical "miracle," no political regime in the world is capable of changing the basic nature of man. No good intention or New Year's resolution is strong enough. All we have to do to convince ourselves of that fact is to read our history books. People of every age, race, and political ideology have contended with the same evils—evils which stem from our own natural propensity toward sin. We are members of a fallen race, and we'll never make it to "holy" under our own steam.

Only by the grace and power of Jesus Christ can we begin to change from the inside out. Only His Light—His supernatural life-force which contains the resurrection power of His Holy Spirit—is able to invade and begin the gradual transformation of one surrendered heart at a time. It's our only hope!

A little at a time over the last eleven years, the Lord has been teaching me to see holiness through His eyes. And it is anything but boring! In fact, most of the time it feels downright risky. To allow the Light of Christ to start a work of holiness in us means that He will begin gradually to separate us from the world and its values. Like the sun at the center of the universe, He begins to draw us into an orbit that revolves around Himself. With all the magnetism of His love, He starts lining up our jumbled motives and values as a magnet lines up shreds of metal. And as He is drawing us into His own powerful energy field, He is simultaneously drawing us away from the powerful pull that sin once had on us.

The lovely, freeing part of this revelation is accepting the fact that we can't achieve holiness on our own. What's more, we're not even supposed to try; we are told that the Lord will accomplish it in us (Phil. 1:6, Ps. 138:8). As Hannah Whitall Smith says in her classic work, *The Christian's Secret of a Happy Life,* "man's part is to trust, and God's part is to work."[6] (And if you're anything like me, you'll admit He has His work cut out for Him!)

The person who most exemplifies holiness to me is Mother Teresa of Calcutta. (By now you may have noticed that she is one of my heroes!) Those who have spent time with her say that she moves through her days in tireless service for others, enduring a mind-boggling schedule and a workload that would exhaust women half her age. Yet she does it all with energy, humor, and a very matter-of-fact attitude. The most striking thing about this petite servant of God is her unself-consciousness. She is so obviously absorbed with the needs of others that she is totally set free from any trace of preoccupation with self.

As God works within us to make us holy, we become other-centered. We need only stay in a close personal relation with Him for this to happen. We need not be overly concerned with what He is doing in us. He has promised to undertake this process of transforming us, and He *will* accomplish it. To focus on "how we're doing" in the holiness department is entirely counter-productive, for any self-focus leads to self-involvement—a very unholy state! If we keep digging up the little seed of holiness to see how it's progressing, it will never grow into a plant. We must leave it in the rich soil of God's love.

When the Light of Christ has done its work in us for a season, I suspect we'll look up one day and see ourselves reacting in a way that is very uncharacteristic of us and very much like Him. Then something in us will feel surprised and excited. We may even ask, "Was that me?"

The answer will be "yes . . . and no"—because it will be Him *and* us. It will be His life shining through ours—His Light shining through our uniqueness. And then we'll go happily about our business without even feeling a need to stop and dwell on this wonderful thing that is being formed in our lives—"holiness"!

A POSTSCRIPT

Just in case you were wondering, on 30 December, the day after our book-moving escapade, Spike and I had the joy of being present in the hospital when Laura gave birth to her third child. Here is an entry from my journal:

30 December 1987, 9:45 A.M. It is freezing outside! But here I sit in a toasty-warm, cheerily decorated hospital room with Laura. Right now *I'm* watching the spasmodic readings on a fetal monitor trace the rhythm of her contractions. *She's* not watching anything. (She feels just awful.) Every once in a while she gives me a weak, brave little smile and I pat her hand. "It won't be long now," I say. I hope I'm right! What do I know?

John is roaming the halls nervously, popping his head in every few minutes with a slightly wild look in his eye. "Dr. Chip" is predicting some time around noon.

A baby! A brand new life will be moving from its place of dark confinement out into this room of light and love. Someone who has seemed to be just a part of Laura will be a separate self—amazing!

12:35 P.M. I have been moved into the next room. Only John and the nurses are with her now. She has been pushing hard for almost two hours. I know she is exhausted. We who wait and watch (Spike, [our friend] Marshall, Ramsay [the expectant big sister], and I) can hear the nurse loudly counting the seconds that she must push and then relax, push and then relax. Little Ramsay is more nervous than any of us.

2:10 P.M. Chip came in at about one o'clock to say that the baby was turned and was not moving into place in the birth canal. Chip's eyes were tired and very serious. He said that he was going to try for ten minutes to turn the baby. If it didn't work, he was going to have to do a C-section.

"Pray," he said. "Pray hard."

We prayed. Big time. The four of us joined hands and hearts and spirits. After our prayer, we just sort of sat there in the quiet, waiting, holding on to each other, feeling our hearts in our throats.

Then suddenly from the next room we heard a sound. A beautiful, high-pitched howl. And John's voice saying, "Alright!" And Laura's "Praise the Lord!"

Oh, Father, You are so good! Little David Mason Barr was born at 1:15. Eight pounds even. A light fuzz of red hair and a dimple in his chin. Perfect! Mother and child (father, sister, doctor, and friends) doing well!

As I look back on that emotional day, I see again with clarity why Jesus calls our salvation a new birth. Like Baby David's journey from the dark birth canal into the bright hospital room, it is a movement from known to unknown—an exciting entry into a new dimension of life . . . and Light!

LORD JESUS, we thank You for Your Light, for the wisdom, the hope and the holiness that it brings. Give us grace to seek that wisdom, courage to cling to that hope, and the will to surrender to the work of holiness You long to do in our lives. We thank You, Lord, not only that You have said, "I am the light of the world," but that You have also said to us, "You are the light of the world." Send us out into the darkness on fire with love for You, so that we may draw others from the shadows of this life and into the glorious Light of Your presence. We ask it in Your name. AMEN.

Light of a Million Mornings

I couldn't see the sunshine through the shadows,
I couldn't seem to find a soul to care,
Then in my darkest hour, You touched me with Your power
And when I looked Your light was everywhere.

(Chorus)
The light of a million mornings filled my heart,
The sound of a million angels sang my song,
The warmth of a love so tender touched my life,
and suddenly
the light of a million mornings dawned on me.

I never tried to understand a sunrise,
I only know it takes away the dark.
I can't explain Your healing, or all the joy I'm feeling,
I only know You've come into my heart.

(Repeat Chorus)

(Bridge)
And now that Your glory has come shining through,
Let my light be a candle that will shine for You.

(Repeat Chorus)

Like the patterns in a kaleidoscope, God's patterns in our lives are many *and ever-changing.*

Beads on a String 8
Living the Kaleidoscope Principle

"THIS IS IT," I thought with a huge sigh of relief as I buttoned the top button. "This is the dress"—a periwinkle blue silk shirtwaist that fit like a dream. Mentally I pulled out accessories of my own that I knew would do perfectly. "At last."

Every day for a week I had been rummaging frantically through dresses of every style and description in countless shops, boutiques, and department stores, looking for the perfect outfit for my twenty-year high-school class reunion. I had started out with a light-hearted attitude, certain that I'd find something right away. It was only after I had tried and discarded almost every dress in Mobile County that I realized how important this was to me.

Why did it matter so much? Most of these were people I hadn't seen for twenty years and probably wouldn't see again for twenty more. I tried to be cool and rational about it, but it was no use. I wanted to look great!

Spike had invested his usual amount of energy in his wardrobe for the occasion—he'd had his navy blazer cleaned and polished his shoes. I tried not to let him see how much the reunion mattered to me, but he must have noticed. (The haircut, the manicure, the suitcase packed days ahead.)

"I wonder if Conner Ammerman will be there," I went around the house saying. "I wonder if she's changed. And Judy Rivers— I wonder if she's changed." What I never said out loud was, "I wonder if I've changed. And I wonder how much."

The weekend arrived. We drove five hours to our hometown in Louisiana, left our boys with their grandparents, and splurged by checking into a motel where lots of the old crowd would be staying. I showered, carefully put on my makeup, and changed

into "the dress." As I walked out into the motel bedroom, I realized I was feeling about as vulnerable as an adolescent dressed
up for her first dance.

"Well, how do I . . . Is it . . Am I . . . " I stammered,
fishing desperately for any quick compliment he could throw me.
That was when I saw his face. The look in his eyes said absolutely everything I needed to know about everything. He
reached behind his back and pulled out a tiny box, just about
jewelry store size. In it was a pair of the most exquisite little
diamond earrings I had ever seen.

Spike is not one to give jewelry most of the time. He'd much
prefer to give me books or a new sleeping bag or a ten-speed
bike. But I will say this for the man—he does have a wonderful
sense of timing. And he knew beyond a doubt if there was ever
a time I needed something special that said "I love you," it was
then. And he was right. That night, for me, something spiritual
happened.

A BREAKTHROUGH OF THE HOLY

In His ministry, Jesus had a way of taking tangible moments
like that and infusing them with a spiritual significance that
spoke His love to those around Him. With the woman at the well,
He used the water she was drawing to tell her the mysteries of
eternal life. At the Last Supper, He used the food He was sharing
with His friends to tell them of life and hope and the redemption
that was near. Each time He did this, the realm of the holy broke
through into the natural circumstances of life.

I believe that something sacred broke through for me the night
of our class reunion. There in the generic setting of the Holiday
Inn, I experienced a holy moment! I found in Spike's gift a tangible
sign of a spiritual reality—the reality of his love for me. In response to my insecurity, his gift said, "You're still beautiful." It
said, "Who cares if Conner Ammerman has changed or not
changed? Who cares if you've changed? I haven't changed. I'm
still crazy about you!"

I have come to refer to moments like that as "kingdom moments." And they do not by any means occur only during special
events like class reunions. Jesus tells us in Scripture that the
kingdom is at hand, it is among us and within us, so we should

not be surprised when it comes breaking through into the events of our everyday lives!

Frederick Buechner points out in *Wishful Thinking* that "church isn't the only place where the holy happens." The spiritual can infuse the tangible, creating holy moments at any time. "Watching something get born. Making love. A high school graduation. Somebody coming to see you when you're sick. A meal with people you love. Looking into a stranger's eyes and finding out he's not a stranger." Any of these can be holy moments. Buechner says that "if we weren't as blind as bats," we might discover that all of life is holy.[1]

FINDING THE GLORY

How do we become more in touch with that kingdom quality in our lives? How can we discover the inward grace in the outward sign? Just knowing that it's there is the beginning of what can be a growing awareness.

One of my favorite singer/songwriters is Pam Mark Hall. I love these words from her song "Find The Glory There":

> When every breath is sacred
> And every task a prayer
> And I embrace the smallest place
> And I find the glory there
>
> Find the glory there
> A treasure that is hidden
> He showed me where
> Find the glory there
> By His Spirit it is given
> In the yoke I wear
> On the altar of the common place
> I find the glory there[2]

To see the glorious in the commonplace, to find the holy in the everyday, is the challenge at the heart of our lives as Christ-conscious believers. The perfect light of Jesus is *always* there, shining through the imperfect events and people in our lives. The exquisite patterns of His love are being formed and re-formed, shifted and rearranged like jewels before our eyes in the

small particulars of our lives every single day. The problem is
that we aren't always able to see them.

Last summer I bought a book called *Living a Beautiful Life* by
interior decorator Alexandra Stoddard. I bought it because I was
intrigued by the subtitle, "500 Ways to Add Elegance, Order,
Beauty, and Joy to Every Day of Your Life." Although elegance
has never seemed to me an essential element in a fulfilling life, I
do believe that our lives as Christians should reflect the "order,
beauty, and joy" of the One who has called us into being. (I tend
to buy books with these words in the title since my own life, at
times, falls more into the "frantic, fractured, and frustrated"
category!)

The book by Stoddard is not intended to be "spiritual," but it
does present a compelling idea which is worth considering on a
spiritual level. The author points out that in her work as a decorator, she has noticed that many people tend to invest 95 percent of
their energy and money on 5 percent of their lives (the big wedding or anniversary celebration, the one-week vacation) while
neglecting the everyday events. In decorating, it is this principle
that prompts homeowners to spend the largest share of their
money decorating the living room that never gets used while neglecting the bedroom and bathroom that get used every day.

Can you see Stoddard's 95-percent-5-percent theory operating in our Christianity? How many of us Christians wait for that
one hour on Sunday morning to hear from God, when He's been
trying to whisper in our ears all week long? How many of us
wait for that once-a-year retreat or seminar to give us the super-
spiritual uplift, when God has been riding around in our cars
with us, eating bacon and eggs with us, working at our jobs with
us every day of the year?

100 PERCENT LIVING

The Lord is not content with a 5 percent Christian walk. His
"kingdom moments" are always waiting to break through into
the special as well as the ordinary events of our lives, for He is
with us, near us, operating in 100 percent of our lives. ("Lo, I am
with you always . . ." Matt. 28:20.) The challenge for us is to
become increasingly more conscious of that fact. Our willingness and ability to tune in to Him in our midst, to become aware

of Him who is "over all and through all and in all" (Eph. 4:6) will radically change our lives. The more aware we are of Him in everything, the more we are able to love Him as He has commanded us to—with all of our heart, all of our soul, all of our mind and all of our strength" (Mark 12:30).

When we live only for those 5 percent peak moments (whether planning for the future ones or looking back nostalgically to those in the past), we are robbing ourselves of 95 percent of our lives. Looking forward or backward denies us of today, the only day we ever truly possess. One way for us to experience the kingdom more fully is to value the here and now and all that it has for us.

My Dad is an incurable optimist. One Father's Day I had a T-shirt made for him bearing his favorite slogan, "Never had a bad day in my life!" (We used to know when things had been really stressful for Dad. He would come in and say, "Well, I almost had a bad day today!")

Once my parents were in a small group at church in which each group member was asked to chart his or her "life line" on a piece of paper. Peak moments such as marriage or college graduation were to be noted by a rise in the line, whereas a drop in the line was to indicate difficult times such as a serious illness or the death of a loved one. Mama reported to us that Daddy carefully drew his life line beginning in the lower left-hand corner of the paper and progressing diagonally upward, ruler straight, to the upper right-hand corner, without a single dip or curve. He really feels that way about life—all of it!

One morning last August, while I was visiting my parents, Dad and I got up early and had a wonderful conversation out on the patio before anyone else was awake.

"You know," he told me, "I believe this year is the best year of my life." I was frankly surprised. Dad is seventy-five years old, has developed a severe hearing loss, and like everyone else in the oil industry, has had some serious financial setbacks in recent years.

"Why do you think *this* year is the best, Dad?" I wanted to know.

"Well," he began, "I just love my work and the people I work with. And it's a thrill to see how my grandchildren are turning out. And your Mama and I have never been happier." He went on for several minutes describing all the reasons he has now to be

more excited about life than he ever has been before. They were
not grand or impressive reasons. They were the reasons of a man
who is experienced at finding joy in the here and now. I was
reminded of Paul's words to the Philippians: "I have learned the
secret of contentment in every situation" (Phil. 4:12, LB).

Dad could be looking back to years when his business was
thriving or when he had the excitement of working in national
politics as State Republican Chairman. Or he could be looking
forward to the time when the oil-related work in this country
will be back on the rise. But both of those points of view would
surely rob him of the "kingdom moments" he is discovering all
around him in people and things exactly as they are today.

There is nothing in our past or our future more important than
this moment in God's presence. Life is far more than a rehearsal
for heaven. It is a gift of the holy, full of grace and power.

But how can we access that reality in our everyday lives? I have
found it helps to think of my moments as beads on a necklace.

THE ADD-A-BEAD PERSPECTIVE

Remember the add-a-bead necklaces that were so popular
several years ago? You bought a little chain with a special clasp,
and then you added beads of various kinds one by one. And if
you wanted to, you could take off all the beads and restring them
in a different pattern or combination.

Sometimes I think of each separate moment of the day—each
event, occurrence, conversation, job, activity, whatever it is—
as a "bead" the Lord has given me. Some may be perfect pearls
(the birth of a child, a rare moment of heart-to-heart communication with someone I love). Most are fairly plain—not even
semiprecious (a rainy-day carpool full of noisy, wet little boys,
a confrontation with a co-worker). Some are rough-cut gems
that may require a lifetime of handling, of turning over and
over in prayer, to bring out the deep and hidden beauty of
God's will (the deaths and difficulties, the heartaches and
struggles).

There are days when these pearls and gems and many-
colored "beads" happen so fast, they pile up around me in a
disorderly jumble. Only in quiet times of prayer, with God's
help, am I able to sort through them, polish and arrange them.

Then with His guidance I can decide which of several different strands to string them on.

Each goal and purpose in my life is a different strand. My home and family is one; my work (the expression of my gifts), another. My personal relationship with the Lord, the Christian community of which I am a part, my outreach to the world—each is a strand upon which I string the "beads" of my days' activities.

At the end of a hectic day, when none of my efforts has seemed particularly meaningful, I can ask the Lord to help me sort through the jumble of activities and add each bead that fits to one of these strands of meaning in my life. Even the most mundane of duties in my day can gain new significance when I see that it has added in some way to one of my purposes or goals. If I have paid my bills, that bead goes on the household strand. If I have met with a child's teacher or run an errand for my husband, that bead is added to the family strand. If I have had thirty minutes alone when I took the phone off the hook and curled up in bed with my Bible—that I add to my friendship-with-the-Father strand.

Some days it seems that the family gets all the beads and the Father gets neglected. Some days I can't find a minute for my writing because the hours have fallen prey to the urgent and the trivial. But I can keep track this way. And if things are getting way out of kilter, I can try to concentrate more on the strands that need beads!

Though in reality the strands of my life are closely wound together, it is helpful for me to separate them mentally in this way, so that I can see the different, interrelated facets of who I am and how my life is shaping up. It helps me, too, to remember that every part of every day (every "bead" on every "strand") is somehow holy. I can see every event as an outward sign of inward grace, for even as we are filled with Him, so is all of life infused with His glory.

How can we become more awake to and aware of this kingdom quality of life? Are there ways of opening up more to God's presence? Ways of living more transparently? Ways of drawing the small pieces of our lives more and more into His transforming light?

As I look at what I consider the major strands of my life as a Christian, I want to share with you some of the ways of living out this kingdom quality—ways that have become part of my spiritual journey.

Not all are alike—some are concepts, some are "how tos," some are ideas for Scripture study or book recommendations. Each is presented simply and straightforwardly—a single "bead" you can either choose to ignore or string onto your own "necklace"— whatever works for you. In fact, you will probably want to "pick and choose" those you want to read, browsing through this chapter rather than reading it in one sitting.

I hope you can find among these suggestions some ideas that help you live out the kaleidoscope principle in your own set of circumstances:

STRAND ONE:
YOUR RELATIONSHIP WITH THE LORD

Meeting with the King

● *OPEN THE DOOR.* Everyone talks about establishing a "personal relationship" with Jesus Christ. Sometimes, though, it's difficult to know exactly where to start. I believe that the beginning point is as simple as giving the Lord a chance to "get His toe in the door" of our lives.

The book of Revelation pictures Jesus as standing at the door of our hearts and knocking: "Behold, I stand at the door and knock; if any one hears My voice and opens the door, I will come in to him, and will dine with him, and he with Me" (3:20).

Like most Southerners, I had always prided myself on my hospitality—on making our guests feel as comfortable and welcome as possible. When I finally realized how long I had kept the Lord waiting outside in the cold, I felt heartbroken. This was the song I wrote:

IS ANYBODY HOME?

My house was old and shabby, hardly looking at its best;
I was home alone that day, not waiting for a guest.
I saw a Man climb up the stairs and knock upon my door;
I didn't go to answer it, and so He knocked once more.

Is anybody home? His voice I recognized;
I watched Him through the window, and love shone in His eyes.

Is anybody home? He gently knocked again.
He'd stood there many times before, but I'd never let Him in.

This shabby heart I call my home was such a mess inside;
I didn't want my Visitor to see the life I hide,
And so I'd never answered, though He'd often come this way,
But as He stood outside this time, once more I heard Him say,

Is anybody home? No, please don't feel ashamed.
I only want to be your friend; you know that's why I came.
Is anybody home? He gently knocked again.
My hand was trembling as I turned the key to let Him in.

I tried to keep Him in the rooms where I had cleaned a bit;
He only smiled and asked me if I'd show Him all of it,
And as He moved from room to room, I had to stop and stare,
For every room He entered, He left peace and order there.

Is anybody home? My doors are open wide.
There're flowers in the windows and a welcome mat outside.
Is anybody home? Lord, I never knew before
The miracle of You begins with opening a door.[3]

● *OUR HEAVENLY DADDY.*   Enter into an intimate relationship with God as your "heavenly Daddy."

John Wimber has described prayer as "intimacy with God."[4] But it is difficult to be intimate with someone you don't know well, someone you're not even certain that you trust. That's why it's especially meaningful to know that Jesus spoke to God as "Abba," which is often translated "Father" but really means "Daddy"—it was the term Hebrew children used for their fathers. Our prayer lives will never be as richly rewarding as they could and should be until we learn to communicate this intimately with God.

Now for some of us, a painful relationship with our earthly fathers can make it hard to relate intimately with God as our Father. Recently my friend Lori experienced a spiritual breakthrough. She realized that she had been expecting God to give up on her any minute and turn His back on her the way her own father did when she was a teenager. Once she understood why she had been mistrusting God, she could ask Him to heal her image of Him (as well as her feelings toward her earthly father).

No matter what kind of earthly father we have had growing

up, we need to see and receive God as our "Abba" who loves us unconditionally. This spiritual understanding will radically transform every part of our lives.

● *THE OPTIMUM TIME.*   Don't give the Lord the scraps of your life. Set aside some prime time, when you are at your best and most responsive, to meet with Him. I heard someone say just this weekend that the Lord doesn't want our spare time. He wants our precious time!

I have my time with God first thing in the morning because, unlike most songwriters, I am a "morning person." (Ask Billy Smiley of the group Whiteheart. Billy once came to Mobile to do some co-writing with me. He was hitting his creative stride about eleven at night. But alas, my mind had gone into neutral about nine-thirty. We had a hard time making music!)

Fortunately our God "neither slumber[s] nor sleep[s]" (Ps. 121:4.) He is both a "morning person" *and* a "night person," so pick any time you're at your best to spend with Him.

● *A PLACE APART.*   Find a special place to meet with the Lord. Though there will be days you decide to vary your routine, it is good to have a specific time and place set apart for prayer. Here are a few ideas on creating it:

(1)   Unplug the telephone or take it off the hook. Pull the curtains. Remove as many distractions as possible before you begin.

(2)   If you have young children, you may have to get up a little earlier or wait for their nap time. If you work outside of the home and have children also, you are juggling a number of obstacles. Just remember, "with God, nothing is impossible!" He will help you find that time and place. He wants it to happen even more than you do.

(3)   Sometimes it is helpful to "set the scene"—especially if you are a person who responds to your senses. Spread out your favorite afghan on your special chair. Light a candle. Make the surroundings welcoming for your meeting with the Lord.

(4)   Get comfortable (comfortable enough to feel "settled in," but not so comfortable that you fall asleep!).

(5)   Gather all materials so you won't have to get up. (I keep

my Bible, study guide, journal, pens, and extra paper in a "totable" basket so they can easily be transported from place to place.)

(6) Keep a little tablet handy to jot down one- or two-word reminders as those "urgent" things pop into your head. If the thought comes to me that I need to call Aunt Joyce, I will jot down "Aunt Joyce" on my tablet. Then I can return to my prayers without further distraction. Often when someone enters our thoughts during prayer time, the Lord is bringing them to mind for a reason. (You might also need to jot down "pick up laundry" or something similar, just to get the thought out of your head. Better to write it down and forget it than to waste your whole quiet time with the thought of laundry intruding on your prayers!)

● *ADVENTURES IN PRAYER.* Be sure to buy and read Catherine Marshall's little masterpiece, *Adventures in Prayer.*[5] In a little more than a hundred pages, she describes eight different kinds of prayer. There may be more scholarly books on the subject, but none more accessible or practical. I learned a lot about prayer from this book.

● *ASK JEHOSHAPHAT.* Read the twentieth chapter of 2 Chronicles; it contains many valuable clues on how to pray when times are tough. These are some I have noted:

(1) When the enemy comes against you, seek the Lord (v. 3).

(2) Fast (v. 3).

(3) Gather your community of believers to seek the Lord with you (v. 4).

(4) Magnify the greatness of the Lord (v. 6).

(5) Recall the ways that the Lord has worked in your behalf in the past (v. 7).

(6) Cry out to the Lord when you're in trouble (v. 9).

(7) Admit to the Lord that you are powerless without Him (v. 12).

(8) Keep your eyes turned to God when you don't know what to do (v. 12).

(9) Bring your family into your prayer with you (v. 13).

(10) Listen to the Spirit of the Lord (v. 14).

(11)   Do not be afraid, for the battle is not yours but God's (v. 15).

(12)   Follow whatever instructions the Lord gives you (v. 16–24).

(13)   Do not be afraid to face your enemy. Stand still and watch the Lord work (v. 17).

(14)   Humble yourself before the Lord (v. 18).

(15)   Stand up and praise Him with a loud voice (v. 19).

(16)   Believe in the Lord and trust His Word (v. 20).

(17)   Sing praises to the Lord *before* the battle (v. 21).

(18)   Enjoy the benefits of God's victory (v. 25).

(19)   Praise and bless the Lord for His victory (v. 26).

(20)   Rejoice (v. 27–28).

(21)   Rest (v. 30).

● *FOR SLOW STARTERS.*   "Jump start" your praise motor with Psalm 103. It literally commands the soul to praise: "Bless the Lord, O my soul; and all that is within me, bless His holy name" (v. 1)! This Psalm loosens up the spirit and lifts the heart, and soon the praise is flowing in our own words!

● PRAISE POWER.   Scripture suggests that we praise God in all things (1 Thess. 5:18). Praise is powerful, for God inhabits our praises and goes to work swiftly in every situation for which we are willing to praise Him.

In our church we sing a chorus called "There's New Life in Jesus." The source of the song is unknown, but whatever anonymous Christian wrote it communicated a valuable truth in verse four, which says, "Allelu is good for you!" It certainly is!

● *JOYFUL NOISE.*   Devote your entire prayer time one morning to singing. I love to do this, though I try to pick a morning when I'm the only one home! I sing and sing all of my favorites. (I keep a little list handy to jog my memory.) I really think about the lyrics as I go, and I make a point to enter into the time as worship.

● *"WASTE TIME" WITH GOD.* If you are thwarted by a "work ethic" mentality when it comes to prayer—if you feel guilty any time you are just sitting still—then you need this tip. Make a specific *choice* to "waste time" with God.

I learned this helpful attitude in 1981 on a silent retreat directed by Francis Vanderwall. Vanderwall suggested that we totally release ourselves from the need to "accomplish" or "achieve" anything during our prayer time. Just as we give ourselves permission to stop work and have lunch with a friend or visit with a loved one, we can *choose* to settle down in the freedom of just being with God.

● *THE STILL, SMALL VOICE.* Reread 1 Kings 19 where Elijah discovers that the voice of God is not a fire or an earthquake, but a gentle whisper. Then practice listening!

● *DEALING WITH FEELINGS.* Don't try to ignore or cover up your feelings with God. Let Him help you deal constructively with them.

Sometimes I bring a real tangle of emotions into my prayer time. At times like that, it is useless to try concentrating on anything else. It is much better for me to ask the Lord to help me process all that I'm feeling:

(1) I ask God to help me identify the feelings. They might be anger, self-pity, or resentment. I write everything down.

(2) I ask Him to help me understand the source of these feelings. Who am I angry with? Why am I feeling sorry for myself? What is causing my anxiety?

(3) I confess whatever part of these feelings involves sin on my part. Usually this confession is not preceded by a change of heart. I may still be angry or worried, but by confessing I am agreeing with God that these are sinful attitudes.

(4) I surrender my feelings to God. I tell Him that I am willing to let go of them if He is willing to take them (as He always is!).

(5) I determine to wait on the Lord. I do not *act* on these destructive feelings. I trust that the Lord is now in the process of changing my heart.

Last week, Andy and I had a heated parent-teen conflict just before I was to meet some people for lunch. On the way to the restaurant, I turned into Spring Hill College and slipped into the last pew of the serene little campus chapel. In a matter of minutes—less than fifteen—the Lord helped me to identify, understand, confess, and surrender my feelings of anger and resentment. I was then able thoroughly to enjoy being with my friends at lunch, and later that day Andy and I were able to discuss and reconcile our differences. The Lord is a great "psychologist" and healer!

● *PRAY SPECIFICALLY.*   Don't be afraid to ask the Lord for specific things. God is very specific about what He wants from us, and He invites us to be specific with Him.

As a very new Christian, I felt uneasy asking God for anything personal or specific. (I felt fine about petitioning for world peace, but uncomfortable praying about my lost car keys.) But God hears and answers both kinds of prayers. He invites us to cast *all* of our cares on Him, because He cares for us (1 Pet. 5:7).

● *PICTURE IT DONE.*   One effective way to pray for something or someone is to picture the prayer already answered. Ask the Lord to help you develop your imagination—it can be a valuable "prayer muscle."

When I was first commissioned to write the musical, *Come Celebrate Jesus,* it seemed an enormous task. Then one day in prayer I found myself envisioning the completed musical as it would be when all the words, melodies, dialogue, and orchestrations were complete. I could see the people coming into a large, brightly lighted church. I could hear the orchestra tuning up. I could see the choir entering joyfully, singing parts. I could even see the lonely, sad faces of certain people in the congregation being lifted with new hope as they heard the music. Though most of the work of the musical still remained to be done, that morning I knew it would be finished!

● *LISTEN TO YOUR DREAMS.*   If you have a particularly vivid dream, write it down. Then, in your prayer time, ask the

Lord to help you understand it. It is not important to decipher every symbol. The important thing is that with God's help we can know ourselves better by paying attention to our dreams.

Once I dreamed I was driving down the street with two garbage cans in the back seat of my car. As I drove along, people would come out of their houses to dump their garbage in my back seat. My car was dragging the ground from all the extra weight. I awoke from this dream feeling very upset.

With a little help from the Lord (and my Mom!), I figured the dream out. Like the car in my dream, I had been extremely overloaded. My overload was not garbage, but work and worry. It was time for me to learn to say no to some of the responsibilities people had been "dumping" on me.

Now, not every dream is this easy to figure out. But I believe that most dreams, like this one, contain some helpful clues to our inner selves.

Dreams can also be more than clues to the psyche. In Scripture, dreams were usually direct messages from God, and I believe that many still are.

Recently, my sister-in-law Tish was saddened by the death of a family friend. She had not known the state of this man's salvation, and she found herself wondering if he was in heaven. "Father," she prayed, "please let me know if Lamar is with you."

That night Tish dreamed of a beautiful wisteria vine, and there was Lamar, one of the blossoms! Tish said that when she woke up, her whole room seemed to be filled with the sweet scent of wisteria. And she felt sure the dream was an answer to her prayer, an assurance that her friend was indeed with God.

● *WANT HIS WILL.* Don't be so hardheaded about your prayer requests that you miss God's clues about *His* will in a situation. The deepest prayer of our hearts must always be, "Thy will be done."

Once my friend Laura was praying for healing for our dear brother Jap Hunt, who was in the hospital. Every time she would bring Jap before the Lord in prayer, she got a picture in her mind of a massive leather book closing. Again and again she tried to pray for Jap's healing, and each time she saw this beautiful book closing in her mind.

Since she did not completely understand the meaning of this

inner vision, this is the prayer Laura prayed: "Father, I know that You can heal Jap, and You know his healing is the desire of my heart. But more than anything else, I want Your will for Jap now. I thank You for his seventy-eight years of life. Surround Annie and his children with Your love. Help us to support them now. Teach us how to pray as we seek Your will for them."

A short while afterward, Jap died peacefully, surrounded by his family. The beautiful leather book closing was his beautiful life coming to a close. His last words to his wife, Annie, were, "Only joy—remember!"

● *MARY OR MARTHA?*   Go back and read the story of Mary and Martha (Luke 10:38–42). With which character do you most identify? Many times, I must admit, I am a Martha, too busy with my own work to sit at the Lord's feet.

I am so thankful for a teaching I heard on this topic by Martha Kilpatrick of Atlanta. She helped me to see that Jesus was not belittling Martha; He was speaking lovingly to her of priorities. Now when I am very busy and preoccupied and find myself neglecting my time with God, I can hear the Lord's voice speaking to me as He did to Martha: "Claire, Claire, you are anxious and troubled about many things. Only one thing is really important."

Studying the Book

● *SUIT YOURSELF.*   Pick a course of study that suits you and stay with it. There are many excellent daily devotionals and study guides available. To find one, ask your friends or pastor to recommend their favorites. Also, salespersons in Christian bookstores are happy to help you make a selection.

Spike and I rely heavily on Barclay's commentaries for our teaching. I also find myself returning time and again to Oswald Chambers's *My Utmost for His Highest* for meditation. It never fails to challenge me to go deeper with God.

One of my current favorites, by Bob Benson and Michael Benson, is entitled *Disciplines for the Inner Life.* [6] Bob was a special friend of mine and an avid reader. This topical study guide, written with his son, Mike, was released shortly before Bob's death. It guides the reader through selected Scriptures for each day of the week on fifty-two topics (one for each week of the year).

For each week there is also a lovely "invocation" and "benediction," a prayer guide, a hymn, and a cross-section of devotional excerpts from the writings of other authors. I love these excerpts because I'm sure Bob gleaned all of his most cherished spiritual "tidbits" from his extensive library of Christian books. Though I may never be as well-read as Bob was, I can take advantage of this literary tour he has charted through his favorite spiritual passages.

● *A FRESH WORD.*   Try reading a favorite passage of Scripture in a translation you are not used to. See how fresh insights spring to life. Try, for instance, reading 1 Corinthians 13 in the J. B. Phillips translation: "Love has good manners and does not pursue selfish advantage. It is not touchy." The meaning here is so accessible! (Overall, this is a beautiful and poetic translation of the New Testament—worth adding to your library.)

Pam, my Bible teacher, teaches from *The Amplified Bible,* which is excellent for providing additional adjectives and expanded meaning.

● *PRAYING YOUR WAY THROUGH THE SCRIPTURES.*   "Pray your way through" a chapter or book of the Bible. This is one of the best ways I know of to appropriate the truth of God's Word for our everyday lives. Verbal or written prayer can be used (I prefer to write). Here's how it works:

As I read through whatever book of the Bible I'm studying, I stop at every verse that speaks personally to me and write out a prayer pertaining to that verse. I try to make these prayers as personal and relevant to my own life as I possibly can.

Here's an example, using Romans 8. First, read the verse or verses:

> For those who are according to the flesh set their minds on the things of the flesh, but those who are according to the Spirit, the

things of the Spirit. For the mind set on the flesh is death, but the mind set on the Spirit is life and peace (vv. 5–6).

Next, write a prayer in simple, conversational words of your own, pertaining to what you have read:

Lord, it's real easy to tell when I'm living "according to the flesh" by what my thoughts keep returning to—what my mind keeps dwelling on. If my thoughts return time after time to anything other than You, I'm usually not "in the Spirit." Sometimes I get totally stuck on shopping for clothes or redoing the house or something like that. Then, before I know it, I have squeezed You right out of my mind. There's nothing wrong with clothes or wallpaper—I know that. It's just that when they take over in my brain like that, they start competing with You. Father, teach me to live "according to the Spirit." Everything else is dying. Only You are life and peace. Those are the qualities I hunger for! Amen.

● *CHARACTER STUDY.*   Do a study of one particular Bible character. Trace his life in Scripture. Read other books and commentaries on his life. Try to "get inside this character's head" and figure out how he thought and why he did the things he did. In what ways is he like you? Different from you?

● *THE ACTS OF YOUR LIFE.*   Realize that though the Bible is complete, the book of Acts (the story of God's church) is still being "created" in the lives of each one of us who follow Jesus. Write out your own story. Who are you and how is your life affecting the coming of God's kingdom on earth? Don't overglamorize yourself, but try not to be too hard on yourself, either. Make your story as factual and complete as possible. Someday you may be asked to give your testimony, "to give an account for the hope that is in you" (1 Pet. 3:15), and you'll be prepared!

● *CONSIDER THE BENEFITS.*   Go through Psalm 119 and make your own inventory of the benefits mentioned which are available to the man or woman who studies God's Word.

Journaling the Journey

● *WHY WRITE?*   My ongoing, day-to-day relationship with the Lord hinges on the quality of my prayer life. I try in prayer (as in my marriage) not to get in a rut. There are more kinds of prayer than the spoken word. For me, keeping a journal is one way of enriching my prayer life and enhancing my spiritual journey.

Often in spoken prayer, my thoughts are scattered and unfocused. Writing in my journal helps me nail down my needs and understand my own motives and emotions. I frequently "hear from the Father," when writing, as well. The answer to some puzzling situation, the healing insight for some unholy attitude, will sometimes come through the pen and onto the paper as an answer to my need.

A journal also helps me crystallize my own good intentions. When I have written down a spiritual commitment and dated it, it is difficult for me to pretend I never made it.

Every person's journal will be different. Mine is full of doodles and rhymes and all the things that characterize my personality. I have a friend who makes a simple list of needs each day in her journal and then proceeds to pray for each item she has listed. I'm sure there is a Christian secretary somewhere who journals in shorthand! The form is not important in the least. There is no right or wrong way. Your journal should merely be an expression of you. So, write on!

● *ONE WAY TO START.*   Here's a journal format I have found useful (Thanks to Mary Lou and Pam for it!):

Begin with a small, 5 x 7, three-ring, loose-leaf binder. Use dividers for the following sections: (1) Reflections on Scripture; (2) Written prayer requests on one side of the page and how God has answered these prayers on the other (include dates that prayers were asked and answered); (3) Dialoguing with God— what we say to Him, as well as what we "hear" Him saying to us; (4) Insights (use alphabetical tabs for these, so that all revelations about "grace," for instance, would be filed under G).

Or, be creative! Set up your own kind of journal to suit your own inner journey. Then make using it a habit.

Note: As my journal gets full, I move the pages to an "archive notebook" and add fresh pages to the journal itself.

● *LOVE LETTER.*   Another good way to keep a journal is to think of each entry as a letter to the Lord. Begin by focusing on how much you love Him and why. Thank Him for the ways you see Him working in your life, as well as for prayers He has answered. Then tell Him exactly what you're feeling that day—what's bothering you, what you're struggling with, and what you hope to accomplish. Confess where you've messed things up and gotten out of His will. Bring certain people into your communication—your family, as well as whomever else you're concerned about. If you have a busy day planned, go over it with the Lord, praying for strength in hard situations, wisdom in confusing ones, and love for every person you will be dealing with.

● *AUDIENCE OF ONE.*   When writing in your journal, remember that God is your only audience. If you are constantly thinking that future generations may find this document and proclaim you a saint (or even a fascinating sinner), you are certain to embellish the facts just a bit! Find a private place to keep this most private of books, and then be as real as you can possibly be with the Father. He values our honesty with Him above all else.

● *TELL YOUR OWN STORY.*   Rainer Maria Rilke, in his *Letters To A Young Poet,* provides excellent advice and incentive to the potential journal-keeper. General themes, Rilke suggests, should be avoided in favor of those specific and personal details of our own lives: "Seek those [themes] which your own everyday life offers you; describe your sorrows and desires, passing thoughts and the belief in some sort of beauty—describe all these with loving, quiet, humble sincerity, and use, to express yourself, the things in your environment, the images from your dreams, and the objects of your memory."[7]

Rilke even contends that, by writing, we will discover beauty in the ordinary, enriching our lives, however humble they may

be. We all have the making of a story to be told—memories of
the past, its people and places, its meaning to us; commitments
and occupations of the present; and hopes, dreams, and prayers
for the future.

STRAND TWO:
YOUR HOME AND FAMILY

Keeping a Home

● *THE HOME AS A MINISTRY.*   What greater blessing could
there be in this unsettled world than a Christian home? God
creates Christian homes not only to bless those who live there,
but as little "outposts of heaven" for weary travelers in this
world. Begin thinking of your home in this way.

The next time you have friends over for dinner, for instance,
pray over your guest list and over all the arrangements. Ask God
to use this setting to work in the lives of those who are gathered.
The Holy Spirit is much freer to work where a groundwork of
prayer has been laid.

Christian songwriter Dawn Rodgers considers her home a
"ministry"—a place where she delights to serve each guest as
though she were serving Jesus!

Our dear friends Clark and Eleanor Akers also have a gift of
hospitality which has been extended to me freely over the past
ten years. There is a constant coming and going of houseguests
in their beautiful Nashville home. No matter when or how often
I show up on their doorstep, I'm made to feel comfortable and
welcome.

● *BLESS THIS HOME.*   When you are moving into a new
home, it is wonderful to gather a group of Christian friends and
give the house an official "blessing." Walk through the rooms,
claiming each space for the kingdom of God, praying for each
adult and child who will be living there, binding Satan, and
asking for a special anointing from God's Spirit.

We have lived in our home for fifteen years, and I am still
saying these kinds of prayers in it! When the atmosphere seems

unsettled, I sometimes walk from room to room, silently asking the Lord to transform the "spiritual climate" by the power of His Spirit. It is amazing what a calming effect this can produce, regardless of the circumstances!

● *OPEN HEART.* Be sure to add Karen Mains's excellent *Open Heart, Open Home* to your library. One of the most helpful concepts in the book is the author's distinction between "entertaining" (which draws attention to the hostess) and "hospitality" (which focuses on the guest).

● *ISLAND OF PEACE.* I remember years ago reading an article by Ruth (Mrs. Norman Vincent) Peale. She defined homemaking as creating an island of peace in a sea of confusion.

It helps me to remember that I serve a God of order and peace. When things are hectic around the house, my prayer is often, "Lord, draw order from the chaos. Just as You did when You created the world, create order within these walls."

Building a Family

● *THE MOOD SETTER.* We wives and mothers have the privilege and the responsibility of setting the mood for our whole household. If you don't believe it, check it out in your own house today. If we deal cheerfully with the daily problems and conflicts that arise, the general mood of the family will follow our lead. If we allow small things to get us down and make us irritable, the family attitude will generally follow suit. For this reason, we have a responsibility to ourselves and those around us to stay positive as much of the time as possible. Here are some things I do to try to keep myself a "sunny" mood-setter:

(1) Exercise is a terrific mood-lifter. Researchers at the National Center for Health Statistics conducted a recent survey of more than seventy-five thousand adults on the mental benefits obtained from exercise. This was their conclusion: "The more consistently people exercise, the better their mental health."[8]

I remember a time, when I was in a particularly grouchy

mood, when Curt went and got my running shoes and handed them to me without saying a word. I got the "message," took the run, and felt 100 percent better!

(2) Plan a space in your week for a good visit with an encouraging friend—someone with whom you can really be yourself. A heart-to-heart talk is the best therapy in the world for a sagging spirit!

(3) Surround yourself, whenever you get a chance, with people who are "uppers." These are people who make you feel positive, people who genuinely care about you. They will fuel you for the "down" situations and people who come into your life, needing your spiritual energy.

(4) Have an "at home" project that you find really fun and challenging. My friend Christine, who has six children (five are under eight years old!), bakes bread for the pure pleasure of it. She says it renews her and gives her a fresh outlook.

(5) When you feel a bad mood settling over you, try to trace it back to its source. Did you feel rejected in some situation or slighted by some comment? Stop where you are and ask the Lord to give you insight into the situation. Perhaps you will see that you were being super-sensitive. Or you may need to forgive someone or ask someone's forgiveness.

(6) Claim the fruits of God's Spirit. These are ours by virtue of His indwelling life. It helps me to go over the list in Galatians 5:22 and remind myself that each of these qualities—love, joy, peace, patience, kindness, goodness, faithfulness, gentleness, and self-control—is already mine in Christ.

(7) Realize that sometimes our gloomy moods are brought on by the subtle "attacks" of our enemy. Satan is the accuser of the brethren (Rev. 12:10). Some of the negative ideas in our minds may be nothing more than his accusations. We can deal with Satan as Jesus did in the wilderness—counterattack by speaking the truth of God's Word.

(8) Don't miss your time alone with God. I can trace many a negative mood of mine to a lack of prayer.

● *FOOD FOR THOUGHT.*   Give your child more than food to chew on. I frequently enclose a note in the lunches I pack for my children to take to school. It usually includes a personal word of encouragement as well as a word from the Word!

Example: "Dear Andy, 'I can do all things through Christ who strengthens me' (Phil. 4:13, [NKJV]). Tear 'em up on your English exam! Love, Mom."

● *DO YOU READ ME?*   Set aside a night a week to read a book aloud as a family, chapter by chapter. My mom always read to us as children, and we loved the suspense of waiting for the next installment on each adventure. This is a great way to share classic literature and quality time with your children. You will love having the TV off so much that you might make it a habit!

My sister Ann and her husband Charlie have always read aloud to each other and to their children. This may be one reason both of their girls are such avid readers now!

● *MOTHER'S HANDS.*   In a 1980 interview with *Today's Christian Woman,* Edith Schaeffer encouraged young mothers to value the small, seemingly unimportant times spent with children, for we never know which moment a child will remember. Often, she pointed out, it is not the birthday party we worked so hard on, but some unplanned-for incident that stays in a child's mind.

Mrs. Schaeffer's own daughter, after she was grown, reminded her mother of a childhood illness when the soothing touch of her mother's hands had been a comfort to her all one night. This was the incident her daughter always recalled when she thought of her mother's love. Interestingly, it was an incident that Mrs. Schaeffer herself had forgotten!

● *MAKE YOUR OWN TRADITIONS.*   Families thrive on traditions. If your family doesn't have any, invent some of your own right away! Your children will love you for it.

One lazy Saturday more than twenty years ago, before we even had children, Spike and I were at his parents' house waiting for our friends, the Wolvertons, to come to dinner. On a whim, Spike decided to ask everybody to wear a hat. That was the inglorious beginning of the now-famous Annual Cloninger Hat Party, which includes a vote for "Best Hat."

Over the years the rules for the hat party have become sillier and more complex. Each person must be able to wear his hat during the entire meal. (One year when my parents attended, Mama was disqualified for a beautiful, but heavy, hat she had to abandon mid-meal!) Each person can make a five-minute speech in support of his hat. Each person has only one vote. (To Spike's eternal disgrace, he was caught cutting his ballot in two and voting for himself twice one year!) No vote buying! (Everyone breaks this rule and shamelessly offers anything and everything in exchange for a vote.) The winner gets to keep the hat scrapbook and the hat medallion for the whole year until next year's hat party.

These absurd rules give you an idea of what a ridiculous and fun evening this makes for adults and children as well. My children have always enjoyed the privilege of seeing their grandparents, aunts, uncles, and family friends act utterly childish on occasions like this. And the silliness does wonders for everyone involved.

Children love to say, "our family always does . . ." The occasion can be serious, sentimental, or silly. Traditions are like glue for relationships. I recommend them highly.

● *MAKING MEMORIES.*   A wonderful investment for every family library is the book *Let's Make A Memory* by Gloria Gaither and Shirley Dobson.[9] It is filled with practical ideas for fun things to do together as a family.

● *ONE ON ONE.*   All right, all right. I know you've heard this one a million times, but that's just because it's so important. Spend some time each week *alone* with your spouse, enjoying time together and really talking.

It's also important to seek out one-on-one times with each child.

● *BE FLEXIBLE.*   Make peace with your daily circumstances —the plusses and the minuses. Make needed changes whenever possible and then learn to accept, even embrace, the rest of it.

Once when my boys were aged two-and-a-half and ten months, we spent a sweltering summer in an un–air-conditioned farmhouse outside of Opp, Alabama, while Spike bought oil leases. I spent every day in one hundred-plus-degree weather with no car, no television, no phone, no friends, and two babies. Spike would get home about eight every night and wonder why I was babbling incoherently to myself.

After a near-nervous breakdown from heat, loneliness, and boredom, I decided in self-defense to stop feeling sorry for myself and teach myself to sew. I went to the five-and-dime in Opp and bought a stack of material—three yards for a dollar. Before the summer was over, that old farmhouse had new curtains in every window and dust ruffles on every bed! I also taught little Curt all of the songs from the musical, *Oklahoma!*, and watched Andy learn to walk.

I never sewed another stitch after that summer. The real lesson I learned was the one about making the best of a bad situation.

I was amazed last year to see how Sandi Patti and the members of the music group First Call were able to adjust to the sometimes-chaotic prospect of living on the road for weeks at a time with their children. Mel Tunney (of First Call) and her talented musician-husband Dick shared with me how they learned to enjoy on-the-road times with daughter Whitney. Rather than focusing on the inconvenience of being away from home, "we have learned to see these times as mini-vacations," Mel said. "Someone else is responsible for the cooking and cleaning. All we have to do, really, is play with the baby during the day and give a concert every night!"

● *UNBIRTHDAYS.*   Have unscheduled celebrations for "no good reason." Life is so "temporary." It makes sense to seize every passing opportunity for joy.

I am very partial to "unbirthdays" (à la *Alice in Wonderland*). It takes very little to create a festive feeling. A cake with candles, paper hats from the dime store, and you've got it. A silly gag gift for each person, wrapped, on each plate, is also fun. Other "unreasons" for celebrating might be:

(1)   Finishing a science project.
(2)   Bringing a math grade up from a C to a B.
(3)   The first fresh strawberries of the season.

(4)   It's Tuesday!
(5)   (You get the idea.)

● *REDEFINE SUCCESS.*   Learn to define your success in terms of family relationships rather than cultural yardsticks such as money, power, and so on.

Our good friend Barry Silverman told me years ago when his children were young, that he was learning to view his personal worth in terms of his role as a husband and father rather than in terms of career and financial achievement. He said that one night, lying on a quilt with his two children in his own backyard and looking up at a sky full of stars, he realized that he was a successful man according to what *he* felt was important, regardless of how the world viewed him.

● *FAMILY HISTORIAN.*   Every family needs at least one. Our brother-in-law Marc Lamkin is a gifted photographer who supplies us with beautiful pictures of occasions and relations. Spike's sister Chigee is a whiz at gathering and cataloguing memorabilia. My brother Johnny is a "pro" with a video camera. In our small family unit of four, the job has fallen to me. I have started scrapbooks for each child to hold certificates and clippings from sports and other activities, as well as photographs through the years. Another tradition I have initiated is a scrapbook for each vacation. In it we file ticket stubs and programs, photos, hotel postcards, and other souvenirs, as well as any poems or writings by family members about the trip. Each new trip we plan is an occasion for getting out the scrapbooks of vacations past.

One of the most enjoyable things I have done as family historian has been to keep a little journal for each boy. I have tried to write in each boy's book several times a year. Sometimes my entry will be about an honor or achievement in that child's life. Usually though, it merely describes my feelings about him and our life together. (For example, "I was proud of you today . . . you are turning into a very thoughtful person." Or, "Someday I hope you'll understand how hard it was for me to make this decision tonight.") When Curt went off to college this year, I gave him his book.

STRAND THREE:
YOUR RELATIONSHIPS OUTSIDE THE FAMILY

Living in Christian Community

● *SMALL GROUPS.* Ask your church leadership to consider forming small "cell groups" within your own church body. The addition of small groups to our church community has opened us up to much new life as we grow together. The kind of intimacy, caring, and accountability available to groups of ten to twelve members cannot be achieved in larger groups or in the church as a whole. Our groups meet in homes one night a week.

There are many excellent books on the subject of small groups. Two of my favorites are David Watson's *Called and Committed* and Anne Ortlund's *Discipling One Another.*[10]

● *HE AIN'T HEAVY.* As brothers and sisters in Christ, we need to hold up one another in prayer—and this applies to your pastor or minister, too! One of the most positive things I've ever been a part of was a support group of ten people who met every Monday to pray with and support our pastor. Often the pastor is the one most in need of ministry and the one least likely to get it. We developed a high degree of commitment, love, and trust within the group, allowing John to openly admit his own fears, uncertainties, and needs. (Yes, everybody has them, even your pastor!) This allowed us to pray with and for John, addressing each need specifically. Incidentally, allowing your pastor to be a human being is one of the most precious gifts you can give him.

● *SHARE THE LOAD.* Find ways to swap jobs or share work within the Body of Christ. Difficult tasks take on a lighthearted quality when there are friends involved. (Remember the old-time quilting bees and barn raisings?)

Last summer our friends Nancy, Jacque, and Chris, along with Spike's brother Curt and his wife Tish, helped us redo the living areas of our home. We rubbed, scrubbed, ripped out, threw away, painted, papered, tiled, and carpeted. What a joy to have a fresh, new beginning, and what fun we had working together.

One of my favorite times of "sharing the load" came a few years ago when we helped Jacque and Phillip move. It was a difficult transition for them in lots of ways, and Jacque had been dreading the move. We, the volunteer movers, arrived at the new house on moving day before anyone else. I'll never forget the expressions on Jacque and Phillip's faces as they rounded the corner in their U-Haul truck. There they saw a profusion of yellow ribbons that we had tied all over every tree in the new yard—and us, their friends, waiting on the front step with a hot picnic breakfast!

● *THANKFUL HEARTS.* Find ways to express your thanks to all those in your life who have been helpful and supportive to you. Everyone thrives on knowing he or she has made a difference to someone else. A simple note of thanks to a friend who has encouraged or helped you takes so little time and means so much. (I remember one Bible study class just before Thanksgiving when Pam, our teacher, suggested that we write to someone special in our lives we may never have thanked. Then she handed out the stationery and gave us time to write the notes on the spot.)

Of course, the One most deserving of our thanks is the Lord. Spike recently spent a week in Alaquippa, Pennsylvania, at The Community of Celebration, a Christian community. One of the many things that impressed him about this joyful group of committed Christians was their attitude of thankfulness. Every worship service was viewed as an opportunity to express thanks to God for the small specifics of their lives, as well as for the grand and glorious blessings He bestows.

Spike was particularly touched by a young man named James who stood in front of the congregation one evening and thanked the Lord for his new clothes, which he then turned around to show off to the group! A truly thankful heart learns to take no good thing for granted. ("Every good thing bestowed and every perfect gift . . . [comes] down from the Father of lights," James 1:17.)

● *CONTRIBUTE TO THE KINGDOM.*   Use your gifts to enrich the life of the Body of Christ where you worship.

My brother Charlie deGravelles is a poet. (His first book of poems, *The Well Governed Son*, was released this year by the New Orleans Poetry Press.) Last Christmas, Charlie used his gift of writing to create a Christmas drama tailor-made for the members of his small Episcopal church in Baton Rouge.

Patti Bass is one of many fabulous cooks in our congregation. Patti generously shares this gift with our membership at church suppers and get-togethers.

Ogden Shropshire, one of the senior members of our congregation, is a master gardener whose yard is an acre's worth of flowering plants and trees right in the heart of Mobile. We never miss a chance to picnic at "Shrop's" as a church or as individual families. In fact, he gets a little miffed if he finds that one of us has taken our children to the municipal park instead of to "Shropshire Gardens"! He delights to share his mini-paradise with others.

Share whatever gifts you possess with your friends and church family. Doing so will surely bless them and you.

Reaching Out

● *NEIGHBORLY INTERCESSION.*   Take a walk in your neighborhood and pray for each problem you are aware of in each house you pass. Cover the neighborhood with a mantle of prayer.

The first time I did this, I was amazed at how many needs existed just within blocks of my home. I prayed for a widow who lives alone, a young mother who has multiple sclerosis, a high school senior who had been admitted to a drug treatment center, and a couple who had recently divorced—and that is merely naming a few! Behind every door of every home there are needs. We are all in need of prayer. Our neighborhoods are the logical place to begin.

● *ONCE-A-DAY MINIMUM.*   Spike is on the lookout every day for someone with whom to share his faith. He prays every morning for at least one opportunity, and he is rarely disappointed!

I went with him one day to get a signature from a family in northern Alabama (he is an independent oil lease broker). The woman he was dealing with was having a particularly frenzied day. She asked the probably rhetorical question, "How do you cope with a day like this?" Spike laughed and said very simply, "Well, I'll tell you what works for me." In the most natural way in the world, he shared with the woman how he tries to let the Lord do his worrying for him so he can concentrate on his work. She said wistfully, "I used to do that, too. I guess I need to get back to it."

There are people in our path every day—salespersons, gas station attendants, waitresses, cashiers, our children's teachers and friends, other parents, co-workers—who need what we have as Christians. We are all evangelists and ministers of the gospel. We may never take a missionary trip to Africa or hand out tracts in the airport, but if we are tuned in to the Lord, He will reveal to us the need in the people right around us. And He will show us natural, un–self-conscious ways to speak to those needs in the language of His love.

● *PEN PALS.* Keep your desk equipped with pens, writing paper, address file, and stamps (buy them by the roll, and you'll have to replace them less frequently). Designate thirty minutes or an hour a week to writing a letter or two of encouragement. This can mean so much to an elderly person or someone living alone, a student away for the first time or someone going through a difficult season. I have reserved one cubbyhole in my desk as a catch-all for things to enclose in my notes—photographs, news clippings, cartoons, etc.

I believe that people who find it difficult to write letters are too concerned about making each letter perfect. They will put off writing until they can take the time to make it long enough and worded well enough. What often happens is that the letter never gets written.

My dad wrote me every week when I was away at college. The letters were not long; in fact, they were quite short. (He's not a wordy type like his daughter!) But they let me know I was not forgotten on the home front.

Don't allow a tendency toward perfectionism to paralyze you when it comes to ministry. Send an encouraging word to someone today.

● *ADOPT A GRANDPARENT.* Find an older person in a nursing home who needs a visitor, and make that home a regular stop in your week. When we moved away from our hometown of Lafayette, Louisiana, I felt that my little boys were missing their interaction with older relatives. So we found a sweet lady to visit in a nearby nursing home. We selected Evelyn (Andy called her "Devilyn") as our adoptive grandparent because we were informed that she had not had a visitor since the late 1950s, when her brother had deposited her there!

Evelyn's body was old and crippled by arthritis, but her mind was simple and childlike. On the day of our visit to the nursing home, we would make a stop by the library, where my children would select picture books to read to Evelyn. She and the children enjoyed listening to me do the reading while they looked at the pictures.

We enjoyed our friendship with Evelyn for over a year, until she became critically ill and was moved. That was the summer we adopted Miss Dulcy, an eighty-three-year-old ex-nurse, who loved professional baseball!

● *BEFRIEND A CHILD.* I looked up the other day and realized that my "baby" is six foot three! So I have extra room in my heart for some small friends. If you have a similar vacancy, look around your church or neighborhood and ask the Lord to lead you to a child who would benefit from your friendship. Just one encouraging person in the life of a child can make all the difference in the world. And when you reach out this way, your life will be enriched as well.

● *FEED HIS SHEEP.* Find a way to begin meeting needs within your community. The Downtown Council of Churches in Mobile, of which our church is a member, runs a soup kitchen called Loaves and Fish which feeds up to two hundred hungry people off the street per day. It is very difficult to hear the gospel over the rumbling of a hungry stomach! Love that meets our needs speaks loudest.

World hunger becomes personal when it has a face. Consider "adopting" a child in a third-world country, supplying money for physical needs and exchanging letters. Our adopted "son" in

Kenya is named Kamau. He is a lovely child with a shy smile. When my children were growing up, we had a little "daughter" from India named Amudah. They loved her letters and often shared anecdotes from them in school.

You can become a through-the-mail parent through such organizations as World Vision (Pasadena, CA 91131) or Compassion International (3955 Cragwood Dr., P.O. Box 7000, Colorado Springs, CO 80933). For approximately twenty dollars per month, you will have the joy of knowing that you have helped to change the quality of life for one child. Your Sunday school class or Bible study group may wish to consider adopting one or more of these children as a group project.

● *BE A FRIEND.*   Value your friendships highly—each one is a priceless treasure, a gift from God!

STRAND FOUR:
YOUR WORK

Finding a Work to Do

● *CAREER SEARCH.*   If you are at the point where you need to develop a career or change careers, trust that God will help you find the kind of work in which your gifts can be used for your good and His glory. He desires this as much as you do. It may involve some preliminary training or schooling on your part, but I believe that if you keep seeking, asking, and knocking, He will lead you into a fulfilling career area.

I have prayed with many friends who desire to (or have been required to) enter the job market after having spent years as full-time homemakers. This can be frightening to someone who feels that she has no marketable skills. The surprising thing is that most of us know much more than we give ourselves credit for. The challenge is to find an area where our interests and abilities come together.

Let the Lord be your career counselor. He will lead you to people, programs, and materials that can help.

While you search, print these verses on a slip of paper and keep them in your pocket or purse:

He helps me do what honors Him most (Ps. 23:3, LB).

Where is the man who fears the Lord? God will teach him how
to choose the best (Ps. 25:12, LB).

● *DON'T OVERLOOK THE OBVIOUS.*   Sometimes when we
are seeking work to do that will be fulfilling, we overlook the
thing that is most obvious. Why? Because it seems too easy, and
we think that "real work" should be hard. I have found that
when we are using our gifts, the work will come so naturally to
us that it will seem easy even when it is hard!

My brother-in-law, Curt Cloninger (for whom our son is
named), has always been happiest on stage. I directed him in a
production of a grammar-school musical, *Johnny Appleseed,*
when he was eight years old, and he's been in the spotlight ever
since. But Curt was well into adulthood before he was fully
convinced that he should concentrate on performing his wonderful one-man Christian dramas as a full-time profession.
With some encouragement from his wife, Tish, he made that
decision about five years ago. It is still amazing to Curt that he
can spend his life doing something that he does so naturally
and that makes him so happy!

Christian singer Mark Lowrey is a natural-born funny man. By
his own admission, while growing up he was in constant trouble
with teachers for making classmates laugh during school. He
called me this morning from Louisiana, where he was on the road
with the Jerry Johnston crusade. Mark's job in the crusade is to
go into high schools and make kids laugh before Jerry gives his
more serious message.

"I can hardly believe what the Lord has me doing," Mark told
me. "My job nowadays is to go out onstage and do the exact same
thing that used to get me kicked out of school when I was a kid!"

● *MAKE GOALS.*   Ask the Lord to help you set some large
and small goals for your work. Try to get a sense of where you
are going. Goals infuse our lives with the excitement of focused
meaning. They propel us toward our highest purposes. More
important, they move us out of the realm of the general and into
the dynamics of the specific. If our highest purpose is to further
God's kingdom on earth, God will help us find *specific* ways to

use our own particular gifts and abilities to bring about this purpose. These specifics will be our goals.

"My goals," wrote educator Mary McLeod Bethune in her unpublished *A Spiritual Autobiography,* "were the unifying ideas of my life, and I was willing to go through whatever life brought me in order to reach my goals."[11] It is that kind of "unifying ideas" we all need in our lives and work.

Working to His Glory

● *WORK THAT GLORIFIES.*   Determine to bring glory to God with your work, whatever it may be—homemaker, business executive, songwriter, whatever.

Cleaning the house to honor God, for instance, certainly elevates the task! Sometimes when housework is a grind, I pretend that Jesus will be our guest that night—for in fact, He will! This never fails to make my work more meaningful.

My friend Stephanie Morris is a gifted artist, best known for her portraits. In them she captures not only the physical features, but the personality, of her subjects. Not many people know that Stephanie dedicates each painting to the Lord. In the corner of each canvas appear the letters "T.H.W.H.I.H.," which stand for "Through Him, With Him, and In Him". While Stephanie is working on a painting, she is also praying for the subject of her work. God works through Stephanie, and her work brings Him glory.

Try not to view your life as divided into the "holy" and the "non-holy." All work performed honorably before God is holy (set apart for Him). Anne Ortlund points out that in the life of Christ, God "made no distinction between act and act. Jesus ate, He preached, He went to parties, He did miracles, He rested— and He said, 'I always do the things that are pleasing to Him' (John 8:29)."[12]

● *BIT BY BIT.*   Learn to divide big jobs into small, achievable pieces. Perhaps sorting out a whole, horrible file cabinet is too much to even think about, but you could do just the top drawer this morning.

When I'm writing a musical, the bit-by-bit technique begins with an outline. Each Roman numeral of my outline centers around one song. I will determine to spend this week on song III and the dialogue surrounding it, for instance. In this way the whole musical begins to come together into a whole, bit by bit!

● *REPEAT PERFORMANCE.*   Almost all work involves a lot of repetition. Housework may be the worst offender of all in this area, but even the most "glamorous" career contains some drudgery.

Ask the Lord to give you a breath of fresh air about the repeated tasks in your work. Learn to see the subtle nuances that make each experience a fresh, new one.

Impressionist painter Claude Monet painted the same bridge dozens of times. Each time he found the slight but lovely variations in season, time of day, light, foliage, and so on. We can fine-tune our ability to observe, discover, and delight in the variety and detail in the particulars of each day's work. Developing this gift will greatly enrich our daily lives.

● *A HIGH CALL.*   Wives and mothers, never refer to yourself as "just a housewife." Whether you work outside the home or not, learn to view your wife-and-mother role as what it is— a very high calling from the Lord, a sacred trust, a ministry. The making of a home is the most honorable of professions.

● *CELEBRATE AS YOU GO.*   It is important in our lives and work that we celebrate our little victories as they come. If we wait for something major to celebrate, we will miss much of the potential joy in our lives. I believe it is the overworked, under-rewarded men and women who reach midlife and look up one day to ask, "Is that all there is?"

A songwriter's work is completed long before the release of the album. By the time the record and printed product are released, I am deeply involved in another project, and the edge is off the celebration mood. So I have learned not to wait to celebrate the completion of my work. When a musical is recorded and I have a rough mix of the album in my hands, I rush home to

Mobile ready to gather a few good friends for a celebration. That is when I'm weary from the work, excited about the results, and elated by a sense of accomplishment. I have learned that is the time to celebrate.

● *BURIED TREASURE.* Reread the parable of the talents in Matthew 25. Plug into the fact that the Lord expects us to make the most out of whatever natural talents He's given us. And that means trying hard to make our work the best it can possibly be!

In songwriting seminars I have led, there are almost always some well-intentioned writers of Christian songs who insist that they cannot change a single syllable or note in their songs because God gave the songs to them this way.

I wholeheartedly agree that God is the giver of songs, but I feel strongly that it is our spiritual obligation to make the most of every gift He gives. We owe it to Him to invest our efforts in becoming the best that we can possibly be at what we do. Rather than "burying" the song God has given us (like the wicked and slothful servant), we should work to make it twice or even five times as good by polishing our writing skills and becoming better writers. Whatever we can do well naturally, we can learn to do better with study, prayer, and practice.

O LORD, help us to seek and serve You in all the relationships and occupations of our lives. Help us to see Your face in every face, to find Your life in every situation, to discover Your glory in the commonplace, for this is the key to a life fully lived. We miss so much, Lord, hurrying through our days looking for the mountaintops. Slow us down. Teach us to find the daily wonder as we create small celebrations with one another in the plains and valleys of our lives. And when You take us to the heights, O Lord, may we find You there, too! For You are the God whose glory inhabits both the mighty and the small. In Jesus' name we pray. AMEN.

The Glory of God

The glory of God is the cry of a baby,
The touch of a mother with love in her eyes;
The glory of God is the bend of a rainbow,
The wings of a sparrow that takes to the skies.

(Chorus:)
And it's here just as near as a heartbeat
And as far as the eye can see,
For the glory of God is the praise in the hearts
Of people like you and like me.

The glory of God is the sharing of moments,
The tears and the sorrows, the joy and the song,
The glory of God is a prayer when we're weary,
A smile when we're lonely, a place we belong.

(Repeat Chorus)

The glory of God is the laughter of families,
The whispers of children, the closeness of friends;
The glory of God is to hope in the promise
Of a love that won't die and a life that won't end.

(Repeat Chorus)

*Like light through the kaleidoscope,
His Light transforms brokenness and* *disorder into beauty and symmetry*

Grace Notes 9
A Conclusion

NASHVILLE, TENNESSEE, 1982

She stood at the kitchen sink, her tears falling a drop at a time into the now-tepid water. How long had she been standing there? She was so tired. Tired of the deep, aching loneliness of living with a husband who didn't love her. Tired of the frustration and inadequacy she felt as a mother. Tired of trying to please the parents who would never be pleased with her, no matter what she did. Tired of feeling like a failure.

Somewhere from a deep distance she heard words she had known once, a long time ago. They were gentle words, comfortable words, words of power and incredible beauty:

> Come to Me, all who are weary and heavy-laden, and I will give you rest. Take My yoke upon you, and learn from Me, for I am gentle and humble in heart; and you shall find rest for your souls (Matt. 11:28–29).

From a place inside herself, she felt a letting go, a release of everything she had been trying all her life to hold together, and she heard her own voice speak a single syllable.

"Yes," she said softly, and that was the beginning of the beginning.

SAMARIA, 31 A.D.

The jars were heavy. The road was dusty but familiar. For a while at least she could lose herself in the walk and in the work.

For a while she could cover the nagging feelings of loneliness and guilt with the comfortable routine of drawing water and filling jars. She had chosen this time of day because she knew there would be no one else at the well. The other women would be in their homes by now, and she would not have to face their scorn and rejection.

She stopped suddenly when she saw Him, then lifted her head deliberately and continued toward the well. This man was Jewish. He would not disturb her, she was certain, for Jewish men did not speak to any women in public places—let alone Samaritan women.

"Would you give me a drink?" He asked. Nothing more. His voice was so familiar that she wheeled around to face Him, thinking perhaps she knew Him after all. She did not.

"You're a Jew. I am Samaritan. Why are you asking me for a drink?"

He smiled. "If you knew who was asking you for a drink, you would have asked me for one instead."

"What are you talking about?" she asked.

"Everyone who drinks your water will get thirsty again," He said. "But whoever takes a drink of the water I give will never again be thirsty. The water I give becomes a well within a person's heart with springs of water that flow continually with eternal life."

Slowly she set down her jug. Her eyes were puzzled, but inside, her heart was racing. Who was this man? She must know more of this water that could quench a thirsting from within. It was what she had longed for so many times. She drew near to Him (John 4:5–30).

PHILADELPHIA, PENNSYLVANIA, 1987

She was drinking again. She looked at the glass with the melted ice cubes and diluted scotch clutched in her own right hand, and she could not remember having taken it from the cupboard. She must have done it. There was no one else here.

He was gone. Husband number two, her mother had called him. Before number one had left, he had talked about divergent interests and "growing apart." He had sworn that there was no one else, that he just needed space. After he was gone, she had

tried to tell herself, "Bad breaks. These things happen. All is fair
in love and . . ."

What had she tried to tell herself? The whole thing was a blur.
But now Jerry had left her, too. Jerry. She could not stand the
shape of his name inside her memory. It had edges like a knife.

The ice made hollow clinking sounds against the crystal tum-
bler. At least she had Caroline. No one could take her child away.
Caroline . . . Caroline? Caroline! Had she . . . was she?

She dropped the glass—ice, drink and all—staggered to her
feet and, reeling crazily, stumbled headlong toward the quiet
nursery. She threw the door open with a crash.

"Mommy? Are you . . ."

"Caroline. Caroline. My angel."

She stroked her daughter's curls and sat trembling at her bed-
side until she heard the rhythmic breathing of her sleep, then
softly shut the nursery door.

"God?" she cried, alone again. "God, oh God!" she cried, and
"Jesus, help me. It's all in pieces and I can't hold on alone. I can't
do it anymore. Could we . . . could we . . . start again?"

JERUSALEM, 32 A.D.

She saw their angry faces;
She longed to run and hide.
Their stones could never hurt her
Like the shame she felt inside.

The stranger knelt before them,
Writing in the sand.
He said to them, "Throw your stone
If you're a guiltless man."

The angry faces scattered.
He turned to her and said,
"Did any man condemn you?"
She simply shook her head.

"Then go and sin no more,
For I do not condemn you.
Go and sin no more;
My power will be in you.
Look at Me, you will see

You're not what you were before.
I trust you; trust in Me.
Go and sin no more"[1] (John 8:3–11).

NEW BEGINNINGS

I would hazard a guess that in every life ever lived, from Samaria to San Francisco, from Galilee to Gatlinburg, there are what appear to be dead ends. There are times when the way forward is blocked and the way back has caved in behind us. Times when the dream we had staked our whole lives on falls to pieces in our hands. Times when something or someone (a husband, a child, a career, a friend?) has let us down. Or worse, times when we have been the ones to let ourselves and others down.

When everything in us feels broken and bruised and hope seems very far away, there is God's grace. Grace that calls us to rise out of the ashes of our own sinfulness and pain and rejection and failure. Grace that empowers us to risk living and loving again:

"Come now, and let us reason together," says the Lord, "Though your sins are as scarlet, they will be as white as snow; though they are red like crimson, they will be like wool" (Isa. 1:18).

Therefore if any man be in Christ, he is a new creature; the old things have passed away; behold, new things have come" (2 Cor. 5:17).

For I know the plans I have for you, says the Lord. They are plans for good and not for evil, to give you a future and a hope (Jer. 29:11, LB).

So I will restore to you the years that the swarming locust has eaten (Joel 2:25, NKJV).

No matter how finished we may feel in life, no matter where we've failed or fallen down, the powerful Word of God contains for us the seeds of a new beginning. No wonder Jesus tells us in John 6:63, "The words that I have spoken to you are spirit and are life"! Our God is in the redemption business, the resurrection business. He is a great God of new horizons and second chances, and everything about Him speaks "new life" to our weary souls. Again and again he calls to each of us to gather all the pieces of our lives and bring them into His healing and transforming light so that He can begin to create from them the exquisite patterns of His redemption.

It still hurts me to remember the times I neglected my two little boys during my self-centered "quest for fulfillment." Just when I should have been taking advantage of those precious, formative years, I was frequently away from home, leaving them with maids and babysitters. And even when I was home, I was often distracted and impatient, not giving them the attention and emotional nurturing that small children need.

Later when my vision cleared, I was able to see the results of my absentee mothering. I began to recognize little behavior problems in my children as natural bids for the attention they had not been getting from me.

How Satan went to work on me then! "Well, you've totally blown it, kid!" he said. "It's too late now. Children's personalities are formed in the first five years of their lives. There's no turning things around from here. You are a worthless, sinful person and a terrible mother. You have ruined your children!"

One of the first and most important spiritual truths that I appropriated as a newly committed Christian was this: Satan is a liar (John 8:44)! I have found that many, if not most, of his lies are centered around this main theme: hopelessness. He will find a million different ways to try to convince us that it's useless to try anymore, that our situation is unredeemable and we might as well give it up! If we believe those lies, he has won.

Thank God, I had Christian friends who taught me how to recognize this voice of hopelessness and how to fight back. I learned early in my Christian walk to confront the lies in my head, just as Jesus confronted the lies of Satan in the wilderness. Here are some of the ways I "talked back" to Satan's lies:

(1) First, I agreed quickly with my adversary (see Matt. 5:25, KJV) that I was indeed a sinful person. But then I added that every one of my sins is covered by the shed blood of Jesus on the cross (Heb. 9:14).

(2) Next, I reminded him that I have become "[a child] of God by faith in Jesus Christ" (Gal. 3:26, KJV). I am "accepted in the Beloved" (Eph. 1:6, KJV) not because of who I am, but because of what He has done!

(3) "Nothing is hopeless," I continued. "I can do all things through [Christ] who strengthens me" (Phil. 4:13, NKJV)! "With

God all things are possible" (Matt. 19:26)! "Greater is He who is
in [Me] than he who is in the world" (1 John 4:4)!

(4)   Finally, I reminded the enemy (and myself) that my children are only on loan to me. They are God's children, and He is
at work in their lives to bring about His purposes. "I have committed everything I do to the Lord. Because I am trusting in Him
to help me, *He* will do it" (Ps. 37:5). I don't have to pretend to be
self-sufficent, for my "sufficiency is of God" (2 Cor. 3:5).

All that year, night after night, I would tiptoe into the dark,
still rooms of my sleeping children to lay hands on them and
pray, "Lord, I claim this child for Your kingdom. I bind away
from him the effects of my own neglect in the name of Jesus
Christ. Fill in the gaps where I have shortchanged him. Redeem
my efforts and recharge my love. Raise him to a beautiful new
life in You. Make him a mighty man of God, an oak of righteousness. I pray in Jesus' name. Amen."

God began right away to answer that prayer. His grace began
to cover and redeem my failure.

Not many months after I had begun to claim those things for
my boys, little Andy, who was just learning to write, proudly
brought me a sheet of paper bearing these words, which melted
my heart:

I LUV
Yoo
Mom
Mu
Yr theu
BeST
MOM
Mu
InD theu WrD

For those who need interpretation, that reads, "I love you,
Mama. You're the best Mama in the world." I went out that
afternoon and had it put in a shiny, red lacquer frame which still
hangs on my kitchen wall. Every time I look at that childish
scrawl, my heart soars with fresh hope. It has become a sign to
me of what the Lord can do. Old things are passed away. Behold!
All things are made new!

TRAGEDY OR TRIUMPH

In the Easter musical, *Now I See You,* which I created with Don and Lori Marsh, I suggest that the main difference between the ultimate sinner (Judas) and the ultimate saint (Peter) is the reconciling grace of God, nothing more:

> Two men betrayed Him,
> Two friends of His—
> One with a word
> And the other with a kiss.
> One took his own life
> By hanging from a tree;
> The other found forgiveness
> At the foot of Calvary.[2]

The major distinction between Judas' betrayal and Peter's denial of Jesus was in how the two men handled their guilt. Judas was destroyed by his, whereas Peter was open to receive the Lord's reinstating grace. Judas listened to Satan's clamoring lies of hopelessness, whereas Peter chose to hear the Lord's still, small voice of hope.

God is calling us into perfection, but we aren't there yet—none of us. We've all blown it more times than we'd care to count. This comes as no surprise to Him who created us. He understands human nature—He thought it up! He has made us not puppets or robots, but people with the capacity to choose. And in the process of our learning to choose Him, many of our choices have gone wrong.

But praise God! He has already made a provision for those wrong choices—"Jesus Christ the righteous; and He Himself is the propitiation for our sins; and not for ours only, but also for those of the whole world" (1 John 2:2).

Last Monday night at our home fellowship group, Lori, our song leader, came in with a huge sack of gold paper crowns for each of us to wear. What a remarkable roomful of royalty we were, sitting around on the floor in our blue jeans and cardboard diadems!

Lori began to share how the Lord has been releasing her from chronic bouts of depression and feelings of worthlessness by revealing to her who she really is in Christ.

"I brought the crowns so we could see each other the way God sees us," she said, bubbling over with excitement. "We're children of the King! Precious in His sight! Crowned in His salvation! He's bought each one of us with a great price (the life of His Son), and He's not about to give up on us—ever! No matter what!"

If Calvary is about anything, it's about this—about God's steadfast refusal to throw in the towel on us, His children. There are no hopeless cases, no lost causes, as far as He's concerned. Again and again, He extends to us His hand of grace, His Spirit of hope. His commitment to loving us is so rock-solid that no failure of the past, no power of the present, no fear of the future can hope to shake it.

"For I am convinced," says Paul, "that neither death, nor life, nor angels, nor principalities, nor things present, nor things to come, nor powers, nor height, nor depth, nor any other created thing, shall be able to separate us from the love of God, which is in Christ Jesus our Lord" (Rom. 8:38–39).

It was several years ago at a Faith Alive Conference in Biloxi, Mississippi, that I first heard the author John Claypool speak. He told a wonderful story about a married couple who had a precious only son. The little boy had been working for weeks at school on a special Christmas surprise for his Dad—a handmade ashtray. The day of the holiday open house arrived, and the boy went to school tingling with excitement, knowing that this was the morning he would finally be able to present the handmade treasure to his father.

As his parents came down the hall to his classroom, the boy stood waiting in the open doorway, the clumsily-wrapped gift clutched behind his back. Suddenly, unable to contain his excitement any longer, the little fellow rushed out of the room to meet them. On the way he stumbled and fell flat on his face on the hard tile floor. The fragile ashtray broke into pieces.

Heartbroken, the child burst into tears. His father, realizing what had happened, rushed to the boy and, taking him in his arms, said, "It's all right. It doesn't matter."

But the boy could not be consoled. He sobbed even harder. It was his wise mother who understood her child's grief. She reached over and took his hand.

"No," she said tenderly. "It does matter. It matters very, very much. The gift that you worked so hard on is broken." The boy nodded his head and began to calm down. Someone understood.

"I'll tell you what let's do," his mother continued. "Why don't we gather up all of these pieces, and take them home, and see what we can make out of them."

Our heavenly Father is like the wise mother in Dr. Claypool's story. He doesn't take our pain or failures lightly. He knows how they wound us, and He knows how much that matters. When He sees our lives falling apart, He suffers with us. But He is always standing by, waiting to help us make something new from the small, transparent, disconnected, colorful, broken pieces of our lives.

SOMETHING FROM NOTHING

Nothing delights God more than to make "something" from "nothing." It is His specialty! How He rejoices to take the pieces of a tragic life and create from them an incredible victory! The story of His own Son is all the proof we need to hope in Him when all seems hopeless.

On a nightmarish day when the sky turned black, an innocent man, a servant-God incognito, was tortured to death. Three days later, death could no longer hold out or hold on. A Life too powerful to be contained broke through all of this world's darkness, radically altering for all time the grim prognosis for mankind. Life is not terminal after all. He is risen!

You and I who believe are what Brennen Manning calls "Easter people." We are the victorious children of a mighty King, created in His image to shine in this dark world.

I love the closing words of the children's musical *Arch the Angel,* written by my good friend Karen Dean. Arch is a guardian angel who struggles to understand the sometimes-complex lives of the ones he must guard. By the end of the musical, Arch, with the help of the other angels, has learned to see the family of God through "angels' eyes." He has caught a vision of a people who are still a long way from perfection but are nevertheless quite beautiful.

They do fumble and forget and fall. But more important, they search and they struggle. They question and they cry. They dream and they dare. And when I see them there in a dark world, the Redeemed Ones, I want to shout, "Look at them! How they do shine!"[3]

I closed my eyes just now and asked the Lord to let me see for just a minute through "angels' eyes" into the hearts of the ones who will be reading this book. I don't know where you are on your journey, but I know that somehow we are kin. I know that, like me, you are struggling every day in a world that is far from perfect. I know that you experience, as I do, the daily frustration of living a life where the pieces don't always seem to fit. I'm praying for you right now, wherever you are, that the Lord would make Himself very real and very near to you today, so that you can find the courage to say yes to His invitation to newness. I'm praying that you will decide now to let Him make something new from the bits and pieces of your life—praying that the dark world around you will soon be brighter because the Lord has begun to shine His life through yours!

FATHER, I THANK YOU for Your Hope that calls us out of our despair, for Your Grace that redeems our wasted years and mispent affections, for Your Love that makes all things new. Bring to our hearts the thrill of a fresh beginning as we gather the scattered pieces of our lives— past, present, and future—and place them in Your hands. We wait expectantly to see the emerging patterns of Your life in ours. In Jesus' name we pray. AMEN.

What a Savior He Is

Sometimes does it seem too good to be true
That God's only Son lived and died just for you?
Is it hard to believe that His love's really there
When in spite of your sin He continues to care?

(Chorus)
I don't know what a sinner you are,
But I know what a Savior He is.
I don't know where your feet have taken you,
But His climbed Calvary's hill.
I don't know what kind of words you've spoken,
But His words were "Father forgive,"
I don't know what a sinner you are,
But I know what a Savior He is.

Sometimes does it seem you've wandered so far
You'll never get back to your place in His heart?
Don't you know that He waits for
the sound of your prayer?
Only whisper His name and you'll find that He's there.

(Bridge)
What we are is not what matters;
It's what He is to us.
Who we are is not important,
It's who we choose to trust.

(Repeat Chorus)

Notes ✾

Chapter 2

1. Kirk Douglas, "Let's Leave Make Believe at the Movies," *Parade*, 23 August 1987, 4.
2. Yorifumi Yaguchi, untitled poem quoted in Doris Janzen Longacre, *Living More with Less* (Kitchener, Ontario: Herald Press, 1980), 20. Used by permission.
3. Susan Annette Muto, *Blessings That Make Us Be: A Formative Approach to Living the Beatitudes* (New York: Crossroad Publishing Company, 1984), 4–5.
4. Sue Garmon, untitled poem from *Souvenirs of Solitude*, by Brennan Manning and Sue Garmon, published in 1980 by Dimension Books, Inc., Denville, NJ 07834. Used by permission.

Chapter 3

1. Carole Mayhall, *Lord of My Rocking Boat* (Colorado Springs, CO: Navpress, 1981), 14–16. Used by permission.
2. Claire Cloninger, "Gathering the Pieces," © 1988 by Claire Cloninger.
3. Quoted in Bob and Michael W. Benson, *Disciplines for the Inner Life* (Waco, TX: Word Books, 1985), 158.
4. Anne Ortlund, *Disciplines of the Beautiful Woman* (Waco, TX: Word Books, 1977), 124.
5. Quoted in Benson and Benson, *Disciplines for the Inner Life*, 126–127.

Chapter 4

1. Viktor Frankl, *Man's Search for Meaning,* quoted in Joyce Landorf Heatherly, *Unworld People* (San Francisco: Harper & Row Publishers, 1988), 62.
2. M. Scott Peck, *The Road Less Traveled: A New Psychology of Love, Traditional Values and Spiritual Growth* (New York: Simon & Schuster, 1978).
3. Nick Stinnett and John DeFrain, "Six Secrets of Strong Families," *Readers Digest,* November 1987, 135.
4. Henri J. M. Nouwen, *The Wounded Healer* (Garden City, NY: Image Books, 1979), 93–94.
5. Morris M. Townsend, *There Are No Accidents in the Christian's Life* (Mobile, AL: The Gayo Foundation).
6. Brennan Manning, *Lion and Lamb* (Old Tappan, NJ: Chosen Books, 1986), 71–72.
7. John Wimber, "Why Christians Suffer," *Equipping the Saints,* 2, no. 1 (Winter 1988):3.
8. Paul Tournier, *Creative Suffering* (San Francisco: Harper & Row Publishers, 1981).
9. Paul E. Billheimer, *Don't Waste Your Sorrows* (Ft. Washington, PA: Christian Literature Crusade, 1977), 51, emphasis mine.
10 Quoted in Billheimer, *Don't Waste Your Sorrows,* 70.

Chapter 5

1. "One of a Kind," from the musical, *One of a Kind*—Lyrics by Claire Cloninger/Music by Ron Harris. © Copyright 1982 by Ron Harris Music. Used by permission.

Chapter 6

1. Gordon MacDonald, *Ordering Your Private World* (Nashville: Thomas Nelson Publishers, 1984), 13–18.
2. Quoted in Benson and Benson, *Disciplines for the Inner Life,* 47.
3. Dietrich Bonhoeffer, *Life Together* (New York: Harper & Row Publishers, 1954), 111.

4. Richard J. Foster, *Celebration of Discipline* (New York: Harper & Row Publishers, 1978), 137.

5. Sören Kierkegaard, *Common Discourses*, trans. Walter Lowie (Oxford: Oxford University Press, 1940), 322.

Chapter 7

1. "Light of a Million Mornings," (from the musical, *Everlasting Light*)—Lyrics by Claire Cloninger/Melody by Mark Hayes and Mark Gersmehl. © Copyright 1986 by Word Music (A Div. of WORD, INC.). All Rights Reserved. International Copyright Secured. Used by Permission.

2. Frederick Buechner, *Peculiar Treasures* (New York: Harper & Row Publishers, 1979), 6.

3. Lyric by Claire Cloninger, © 1985. All rights reserved.

4. Yvonne G. Baker, "One Mother's Prayer," *Today's Christian Woman*, January/February 1985, 38.

5. "Everlasting Light," from the musical, *Everlasting Light*—Lyrics by Claire Cloninger/Music by Mark Hayes and Mark Gersmehl. © Copyright 1986 by Word Music (A Div. of WORD, INC.). All Rights Reserved. International Copyright Secured. Used by Permission.

6. Hannah Whitall Smith, *The Christian's Secret of a Happy Life* (Old Tappan, NJ: Spire Books, 1966), 21.

Chapter 8

1. Quoted in Benson and Benson, *Disciplines for the Inner Life*, 201.

2. Pam Mark Hall, "Find the Glory There." © 1984 Meadowgreen Music Co. All rights adm. by Tree Pub. Co., Inc. 8 Music Sq. W., Nashville, TN 37203. International Copyright Secured. All Rights Reserved. Used by Permission.

3. "Is Anybody Home?"—Lyrics by Claire Cloninger/Music by Tricia Walker. © Copyright 1988 by Word Music (A Div. of WORD, INC.). All Rights Reserved. International Copyright Secured. Used by Permission.

4. Catherine Marshall, *Adventures in Prayer*, (Old Tappan, NJ: Fleming H. Revell Co., 1975).

5. John Wimber, "Prayer: Intimacy with God," *Equipping the Saints*, no. 6 (November/December 1987):2.

6. Benson and Benson, *Disciplines for the Inner Life*, (Waco, TX: Word Books, 1985).

7. Rainer Maria Rilke, *Letters to a Young Poet* (New York: W. W. Norton and Company, 1934), 19.

8. Catherine Houck, "Drug-Free Guide to Mood Control," *Woman's Day*, 27 October 1987, 258.

9. Gloria Gaither and Shirley Dobson, *Let's Make a Memory* (Waco, TX: Word Books, 1983).

10. David Watson, *Called and Committed: World-Changing Discipleship* (Wheaton, IL: Harold Shaw Publishers, 1982); Anne Ortlund, *Discipling One Another: Discipline for Christian Community* (Waco, TX: Word Books, 1979).

11. Quoted in Melanie Brown, "Is It Time for You to Blossom?" *Redbook*, August 1987, 75.

12. Anne Ortlund, *Disciplines of the Heart* (Waco, TX: Word Books, 1987), 39.

Chapter 9

1. From "Go and Sin No More"—Lyrics by Claire Cloninger/Music by Dwight Liles and Denise Liles. © 1984 by Word Music (A Div. of WORD, INC.), Bug & Bear Music, and Paragon Music Corp. All Rights Reserved. International Copyright Secured. Used by Permission.

2. "Two Men," from the musical, *Now I See You*—Lyrics by Claire Cloninger/Music by Don Marsh. © Copyright 1986 by Word Music (A Div. of WORD, INC.). All Rights Reserved. International Copyright Secured. Used by Permission.

3. Karen Dean, *Arch the Angel* (Waco, TX: Word Music, 1987), 83. Used by Permission.